PR
5907
E3

81-175

Eddins, Dwight
Yeats: the nineteenth century
matrix.

YEATS: THE NINETEENTH CENTURY MATRIX

Yeats: The Nineteenth Century Matrix

by

DWIGHT EDDINS

THE UNIVERSITY OF ALABAMA PRESS
University, Alabama 35486

Table of Contents

Abbreviations Used in References

1. W. B. Yeats

    A   *The Autobiographies.* New York, 1953.
    AV   *A Vision.* London, 1962.
    EI   *Essays and Introductions.* London, 1961.
    L   *The Letters,* ed. Allan Wade. London, 1954.
    VE   *The Variorum Edition of the Poems,* ed. Allt and Alspach. New York, 1957.

2. Richard Ellmann

    Masks   *Yeats: The Man and the Masks.* New York, 1958.
    Identity   *The Identity of Yeats.* London, 1954.

Preface

Yeatsian scholarship, after several decades of relative neglect of the early poetry, has suddenly veered back to correct its omissions. Within the last three years, at least four books dealing in whole or in large part with Yeats' verse up to 1899 have appeared: Harold Orel's general investigation of development from 1885–1900; Allen Grossman's intensive study of cabalistic sources in *The Wind Among the Reeds*; George Bornstein's investigation of Shelleyan influences and parallels; and Harold Bloom's extensive and controversial reassessment of Yeats' career, in which he argues the superiority of the early poetry to much that came later. These works, and others, have resulted in significant refinement of the observations of earlier critics, but additional refinement is possible—especially with regard to the development of style and technique in the nineteenth-century verse. Close examination of the actual texture and the underlying stylistic and generic concepts of this verse, in conjunction with the verse of certain predecessors and contemporaries, throws new light on the question of which particular senses of "Romantic," "pre-Raphaelite," "nationalist," "symbolist," and other epithets really apply to the early Yeats; and further defines his place in the nineteenth-century literary continuum.

Another reason for further study of the poetry before 1900 is the need to continue establishing the strands of continuity in Yeats' career. One critic praised Yeats somewhat left-handedly for being "the first man to put a carpet down and then build flooring under it," but it has long been apparent that certain beams were in place well before the turn of the century, and that the carpet itself—though eventually toned down from its original flamboyance—always retains its basic luxurious texture. Critical opinion has, of course, swung completely away from the extreme early position which held that Yeats was suddenly transfigured from an "aesthete" into a starkly realistic "modern." Nonetheless, the dramatic nature of the changes which did occur still obscures for many readers the surprising homogeneity of his poetic career as a whole. My primary focus, naturally, has been on the nineteenth-century portion of that career; but reference has been made throughout to similarities in Yeats' mature aesthetic, while the "Epilogue" indicates some strands of continuity which deserve further attention.

The organization of this book is the result of an attempt to combine two chronologies: that of the major literary "schools" to which Yeats has significant relations, and that of Yeats's own early verse. A sort of crude coincidence makes this combination surprisingly workable. In his earliest poetry (that written up through 1886) Yeats is most directly under the influence of the Elizabethans and Romantics commended to him by his father—in particular that of Shakespeare and that of Shelley. With his introduction to O'Leary and his membership in "Young Ireland" he is forced to choose among nationalistic courses, and to discriminate between the influences desirable and malign of such Irish writers as William Allingham and Sir Samuel Ferguson. After 1889, when *The Wanderings of Oisin and other Poems* brings him attention, he comes into contact with contemporary English poets attempting to define a new English tradition in terms of rebellion against that established by Tennyson, Arnold, and Browning, so that the relation of Yeats to matters Victorian becomes a central issue. Finally, it is through membership in the Rhymers' Club that his direct exposure to the writings of the French symbolists occurs, at a time when symbolism has come to be his own major concern.

At least two qualifications should be entered concerning the influences discussed here. First, it was inevitable that some influences would be too pervasive to fit neatly into the sequence described above: Pre-Raphaelitism is a case in point. The examples of Rossetti and Morris are there from the first, since they had furnished Yeats' father with much of his private aesthetic credo, and could easily have been treated in the first section on "Romanticism." It was thought better, however, to discuss the Pre-Raphaelites in connection with "Victorianism," since their divergence from the late Tennysonian aesthetic has important relations to the divergence of Yeats, and of the other Rhymers. References back to concerns of the first chapter, such as the stasis induced by "painting" in poetry, are duly noted. The second point is that, admittedly, the omission of a study of Pater's works as a part of the early Yeatsian background will seem rather strange; but the comparative approach which is basic to this investigation emphasizes the existence of verse models and the transferability (or lack of it) of specific poetic techniques and archetypes rather than the general intellectual influence of a systematic aesthetic philosophy. Those who wish to study the relation of Pater to Yeats are recommended to see Leonard Nathan's article "W.B. Yeats's Experiments with an Influence," *Victorian Studies*, VI (1962), 66–74, and Bloom, chapter 2.

Certain techniques and poetic tendencies serve as binding forces in the study, since discussion of their various manifestations recurs from chapter to chapter. Easily the most important of these is Yeats' attempt to "dramatize" the lyric—an undertaking concerned with replacing the insipidity and diffuseness of passive contemplation with the immediacy and vitality of a moment of "high passion" such as might occur in some tragic drama. Certainly Yeats himself stressed this portion of his achievement when he wrote in his last letter:

It seems to me that I have found what I wanted. When I try to put all into a phrase I say, 'Man can embody truth but he cannot know it.' I must embody it in the completion of my life. The abstract is not life, and everywhere draws out its contradiction. You can refute Hegel but not the Saint or the Song of Sixpence. . . . (L, p. 922)

It is in the synthesis, in the dramatization of the moment of insight, not in the abstract formulation of doctrine that the presence of "truth" becomes most perceptible. The deepest wisdom has an equally deep emotional component which it is the power of poetry to suggest; Yeats' early attempts to master this power are a large part of our concern.

YEATS: THE NINETEENTH CENTURY MATRIX

I

Drama Versus Picture:
the Romantic and Elizabethan
Background

"WE WERE THE LAST ROMANTICS. . . ." THE
context of the phrase in "Coole Park and Ballylee" leaves no
question of the sense in which Yeats regarded himself and chos-
en contemporaries as "Romantics"; it was a sense broad enough
to include the classical poet Homer, and was centered upon the
choice of lofty and traditionally-ennobling subject matter, as
opposed to the intentional search for the quotidian which Yeats
saw as a dominating concern of many modern poets. As several
generations of scholars have demonstrated, however, Yeats'
earliest verse was also Romantic in the more usual and specialized sense; it obviously derived much of its characteristic tenor
from Yeats' immersion in Shelley and Keats, and in those exotic
and supernatural portions of Elizabethan and Jacobean verse
which had previously inspired the Romantic poets.

The assets and liabilities of this heritage have led, inevitably,
to a deep division between critics. One extreme is found in Louis
MacNeice, who believes that the early Yeats languished temporarily and unfortunately in Romanticism as in the awkward-
ness of adolescence; and another in Harold Bloom, who finds
what is good in Yeats' poetry to be more or less what represents
an organic extension of the Romantic tradition, and what is bad

to be a denial or misleading compromise of that tradition. A part of this disagreement is simply the result of incompatible aesthetics. But another part can be traced directly to a failure to make a clear distinction on the one hand between traits of Romantic style which were stumbling blocks in an almost absolute sense with respect to Yeats' poetic achievement, and on the other the acquisition of High Romantic elan and conceptual scope without which that achievement is unthinkable. Mac-Neice, the practicing poet, instinctively senses an unjustifiable turgidity in the early style, but lacks the literary-historical perspective to see the powerful Romantic archetypes which that style often obscures. And like an almost perfect complement, Bloom brilliantly identifies the "apocalyptic vitalism" of the great Romantics at work in Yeats from the beginning, but fails to make a satisfactory defense of the stylistic texture of those early poems which he is concerned to place near the heart of Yeats' lasting accomplishment. My purpose in this chapter is to add fuel to two fires—MacNeice's stylistic condemnation and Bloom's affirmation of Romantic "vitalism."

The prevailing emphasis on the negative effects of exotic decors and "purple" diction in the early Yeats has failed to lead to careful examination of at least one insidious disadvantage of the Romantic legacy—the tendency toward profuse, static description, manifested not only in extended portraits but in the loading of individual lines to capacity with visually evocative words. Although the resultant type of poetry is a perfectly valid one, it represented an essentially false direction for a poet who would rely mainly upon the force of dramatic speech for his lyrical impact. Furthermore, at the same time that Yeats was under the influence of Spenserian-Keatsian descriptiveness, he was already fascinated by the rhetorical power of Shakespearian speech at its moments of "high passion"; by the dramatic masks which such personae as Coriolanus, Prometheus, and Lucien de Rubempré suggested; and by the dramatic poem itself as a genre. Thus we see emerging early a conflict between picture and speech[1] which was to result in a new "dramatic lyric," and which provides a useful starting point for a study of the forces which shaped the poet in his earliest creative days.

Like many innovators, the Romantics as a group were more conscious of the shortcomings of the tradition which they attacked than they were of its positive values; it is not surprising that some of the latter become unnoticed casualties in the battle for a poetry based upon "inspiration" and "spontaneous creativity." One of the more unfortunate examples is furnished by the syntax of dramatic pronouncement, which had been the especial study of many earlier poets. In the hands of Pope, for example, the arrangement of the sentence for maximum force and rhetorical effectiveness acquired the status of an art in itself. This forcefulness, however, had been directed into a decorous social arena alien to his nineteenth-century successors, who believed that the proper study of mankind was not the correctness and propriety of collective man, but the spiritual grandeur of isolated man, the rebel and explorer. Once the sensitive poet had had a premonition of this grandeur and had achieved a creative mood, the words would come of themselves without recourse to what Keats contemptuously called:

> ... musty laws lined out with wretched rule
> And compass vile.... ("Sleep and Poetry")[2]

Words did come, but they were not always incorporated in the patterns and constructions which would provide for their most effective delivery. The loosing of a flood of imagery in support of grandiose conceptions meant a certain casualness of form at all levels from the construction of the sentence and

[1] I note that Edward Engelberg, in his excellent book *The Vast Design* (Toronto, 1964), has referred to a similar antithesis as "picture vs gesture" (Chap. III). His emphasis, however, is upon Yeats' philosophy of art, whereas I have attempted to stress the concrete literary effects of the tension between painting and drama upon the poet's early works.

[2] *Poetical Works* (London, 1959).

verse paragraph to the progress of the plot in narrative poems. The poet would linger over some external scene which had pleased him, elaborating it with long catalogues of related sensuous delights, or would—as Shelley often did in his Promethean speeches—expand some passing thought into a philosophical rhapsody dependent upon little more than sheer fervor and hyperbolic diction for its effectiveness.

It is characteristic of Bloom's approach to problems of stylistic texture that he fulminates against MacNeice's charge that Shelley "was a careless craftsman, verbose and facile, sometimes vulgar in both diction and rhythm" (Bloom, p. 108) but does not come to terms with the actual questions of verbal and syntactical felicity—or the lack of it—which Shelley's verse raises. The fact that the conceptions presented in *Prometheus Unbound* or in Blake's prophetic books are magnificent, apocalyptic, and philosophically consistent does not mean that the monotonous, prosaic, and strung-out periods in which they are often couched should be exempt from critical attack.

The verse of sensuous elaboration found its greatest exponent in Keats, whose determination to " 'load every rift' . . . with ore" [3] implied the development of a technique not unlike that of the worker in mosaic. The speed and spontaneity of dramatic speech gave way to a curiously static art which met the painter upon his own ground and went him one better, for words could make explicit that spiritual dimension of a vista which canvas could only suggest. Sometimes the subject of a poem seemed to be chosen for its congeniality to this method; "To Autumn," for example, aimed to suggest the essence of cornucopia in a series of portraits of harvest abundance and its personifications. Yeats recognized this predilection for detached images of beauty when he wrote of Keats in *A Vision*:

When we compare these [Keats'] images with those of any sub-

[3] *The Letters of John Keats*, ed. H.E. Rollins (Cambridge, Mass., 1958) II, p. 323.

sequent phase, each seems studied for its own sake; they float as in serene air, or lie hidden in some valley, and if they move it is to music that returns always to the same note, or in a dance that so returns into itself that they seem immortal. (AV, pp. 131–132)

Such a method of composition, whatever its felicities, had certain drawbacks when applied to narrative and dramatic poetry. The Arcadian landscape of *Endymion* proliferated wildly, obscuring character and plot in a luxurious welter of objective nature. Each occurrence of an altar, cave, or bower was the occasion for a sensuously detailed painting which dissipated the sense of the hero's presence and made his surroundings more climactic than his actions. These descriptions represent Keats' attempt to depict the archetype which Bloom insightfully identifies as the Lower Paradise—"the world conceived as an erotic illusion." (Bloom, p. 109) But the very notions of external copiousness inherent in such an archetype were inimical to the art of psychic immediacy which was to be Yeats' forte.

Similarly, in lyric poetry where all was oriented toward the external, it was difficult to convey a sense of the subjective pressure which brought the work forth—the sense which radiated so intensely from the work of a poet like Villon. Yeats mentioned this difficulty in a letter to his father, written in 1913, in which he made Keats' poetry the type of a poetry of "vision" antithetical to the dramatic speech associated happily with Villon and unhappily with Burns:

Of recent years instead of 'vision', meaning by vision the intense realization of a state of ecstatic emotion symbolized in a definite imagined region, I have tried for more self portraiture. I have tried to make my work convincing with a speech so natural and dramatic that the hearer would feel the presence of a man thinking and feeling. (L, p. 583)

The word "region" here is of particular interest; it was the same one Yeats had used in 1889 to describe one of his earliest dramatic poems, *The Island of Statues*, in an unfavorable comparison with the "incident or series of incidents" which comprised "The Wanderings of Oisin" (L, p. 106). Later a passage in "Discoveries" would leave no doubt that the Keatsian vision represented a false poetical direction as far as Yeats was concerned:

> I had set out on life with the thought of putting my very self into poetry, and had understood this as a representation of my own visions and an attempt to cut away the non-essential, but as I imagined the visions outside myself my imagination became full of decorative landscape and of still life. (EI, p. 271)

This was, of course, the wiser voice of hindsight; the young poet, fond of projecting himself into the situation of various Romantic heroes, was more inclined to commence his artistic career by the creation of private landscapes into which one might retreat "from the cares of life" (L, p. 106). At least three distinct examples emerge from the earliest poetry: the romantic Spain of *Mosada*, replete with dungeons and a fecund harvest countryside; the Arcady of *The Island of Statues*, an idyllic woodland filled with pastoral flora and fauna; and the Golden-Age India of "Anashuya and Vijaya" and the various Indian lyrics, characterized by exotica such as Brahmin temples, flamingoes, and peacocks.

The settings are obviously unrealistic, but they have the coherence and dense detail implied by the phrase "a definite imagined region." Time and again the obtrusion of specific natural images for their own sake, or at best for a perfunctory reinforcement of the pastoral atmosphere, gives an odd sense of unwarranted concreteness in an implausible world inhabited by the vaguest of characters. This is especially noticeable in Arcady, where we encounter a plethora of owls, lynxes, and other wildlife. At the opening of the third scene of Act I in *The Island of Statues* for instance, a disembodied voice sings:

> See! Oh, see! the dew-drowned bunches
> Of the monk's-hood how they shake,

Nodding by the flickering lake,
There where yonder squirrel crunches
Acorns green with eyes awake.[4]

This bias toward descriptive painting becomes a more serious matter when it begins to weigh down the speeches of the interacting *dramatis personae*, clogging any sense of crisis and immediacy with superfluous images. Mosada's recollection of her absent lover suffers from this defect:

> . . . In April's prime
> (Swallows were flashing their white breasts above
> Or perching on the tents, a-weary still
> From waste seas cross'd, yet ever garrulous)
> Along the velvet vale I saw him come—
> Feet of dark Gomez, where now wander ye?
> In autumn, when far down the mountain slopes
> The heavy clusters of the grapes were full,
> I saw him sigh and turn and pass away. . . .
>
> *Mosada* (i. 6–14)

Such painting also introduces into the characterization a certain passivity, which is magnified in such works as *The Island of Statues* and "Anashuya and Vijaya" by the scenes of paradisiacal calm which Yeats envisages. Themselves without emotional depth, the Arcadians fade at times into arbitrary receptacles of the atmosphere; Almintor does so as he begins his dangerous search of the enchanted island:

> *Almintor.* The evening gleams are green and gold and red
> Along the lake. The crane has homeward fled,
> And flowers around in clustering thousands are
> Each shining clear as some unbaffled star. . . .
>
> *The Island of Statues* (I. iii. 22–25)

Shakespeare, of course, had mastered the art of making his characters register the atmosphere through which they moved

[4] VE, ll. 1–5. All subsequent citations of Yeats' poetry are to this edition.

as an integral and dynamic part of their own involvement in the plot. In the third act of *King Lear* the aged king becomes the oracle of the storm raging about him, and presents a picture of cosmic disorder which mirrors his own mental disintegration. In the *Autobiographies* Yeats looked wistfully at this control over objective nature, which he believed to derive from temporary Unity of Being:

> Shakespeare's people make all things serve their passion, and that passion is for the moment the whole energy of their being— birds, beasts, men, women, landscape, society, are but symbols and metaphors, nothing is studied in itself, the mind is a dark well, no surface, depth only. (p. 174)

The burden of sensuous description was also borne, in a slightly different form, by the personae of Yeats' early lyrics; for years the poet was plagued by the spectre of a facile Romantic formula which made the poetical force of a passage dependent upon the number of vivid adjectives and evocative nouns which it contained. As a result the connotations of individual sentence units, which constitute what John Crowe Ransom has called "the local texture," became a rich, heterogeneous mixture often damaging to the dramatic force of the persona's utterance. This tendency may be seen in its most extreme form in certain early poems which Yeats wisely decided not to collect:

> Remembering thee, I search out these faint flowers
> Of rhyme; remembering thee, this crescent night,
> While o'er the buds, and o'er the grass-blades, bright
> And clinging with the dew of odorous showers. . . .
> ("Remembrance")

> The giddy bee's complacent croon
> Where long grey grasses bow and bend,
> In all its honey-thickened tune
> Has no word of the sulphurous end.
> ("A Summer Evening")

The sheer tumidity and cloying heaviness of these lines make it difficult to believe that they are the work of the poet whose lyrics exhibit, as no lyrics before them, the quality of "passionate speech"—until we remember that this mastery was artificially extended backwards in the series of brilliant but misleading revisions and omissions which reshaped the collections finally known as *Crossways* and *The Rose*.

Although the early poetry is replete with the sort of sensuous, obtrusive imagery which over-enriches its texture, it is only fair to point out that we may find occasional examples of another sort—imagery less colorful and less sharply delineated but for those very reasons more congenial to the dramatic pose which Yeats would later adopt as the best way of getting his "self" into his poetry. It was the imagery of cosmic process, characterized by the interplay of light and shade and by the suggestion of an animated universe in which elements such as the wind and stars were informed by a hierarchy of mysterious powers. Behind this mode of vision lay Shelley, with his Mediterranean translucencies and Promethean allegories. Earth, ocean, hours, and the other indices of space and time by which we orient our existence were actors in a vast Platonic drama which ran always in his mind and which required a hyperbolic language of fire and air in order to suggest the essential spirituality of the universe and those of its human inhabitants who had broken the bonds of flesh. At the beginning of his career Yeats was not yet ready for such transcendental soarings, but there was already an interest in the play of light as an auxiliary to the confrontation with elementals, and as a correlative of spiritual activity:

> When flash on flash once more the lightning came,
> The youth had flung his arms around the rocks,
> And in the sibyl's eyes a languid flame
> Was moving. . . .
>
> ("The Two Titans")

Almintor . . . .
See, yonder sinks the sun, yonder a shade
Goes flickering in reverberated light.

The Island of Statues (I. ii. 52–53)

More frequently during this period Yeats was interested in diaphanous imagery because it seemed an ideal embodiment for the languorous weariness which fascinated him as a poetic attitude. Indeed, Shelley had sometimes applied his imagery to the evocation of such an attitude:

> The pale, the cold, and the moony smile
> Which the meteor beam of a starless night
> Sheds on a lonely and sea-girt isle. . . .[5]

Such passages as this led Yeats to make an interesting distinction between the precision and concreteness of Keats, on the one hand, and the ethereal vagueness of Shelley on the other:

> It may have been some impulse of his nature too subtle for his mind to follow, that made Keats, with his love of embodied things, of precision of form and colouring, of emotions made sleepy by the flesh, see Intellectual Beauty in the Moon . . . which Shelley thought of with weariness and trouble. The Moon . . . because she only becomes beautiful in giving herself, and is no flying ideal . . . is not loved by the children of desire. (EI, p. 91)

It is obvious from this dichotomy that Yeats saw two possible kinds of languor: that which came from a surfeit of fulfilment and that which resulted from the longing of deprivation. In one sense the "definite regions" of Arcady and India, with their serenity and plenitude, represent the former kind—an attitude conducive to stasis rather than the movement of drama. But in the Shelleyan response is contained the stirrings of a drive *toward* fulfilment which is capable of shattering the languorous facade. After all, the doctrine of the masks which lies

---

[5] "On Death," *The Complete Poetical Works of Percy Bysshe Shelley*, ed. T. Hutchison (London, 1934). All subsequent citations of Shelley are to this edition.

at the heart of Yeats' aesthetic theory would be founded upon
the principle that the activity of reaching for antithetical personality as a means of personal fulfilment has a component of
poetic animation.

In his unceasing analysis of the relationship between imagery
and dramatic force Yeats was to discover not only the usefulness of Shelleyan vision, but the necessity for "occasional
prosaic words" if the poet were to escape distracting kaleidoscopic effects. In "Dramatis Personae" he notes that although
such effects have their appropriateness in Romantic and Neo-
Romantic fantasy, they obstruct the sense of the personae's
immediacy:

> In dream poetry, in *Kubla Khan*, in *The Stream's Secret*, every
> line, every word, can carry its unanalysable, rich associations;
> but if we dramatize some possible singer or speaker we remem-
> ber that he is moved by one thing at a time, certain words must
> be dull and numb. Here and there in correcting my early poems
> I have introduced such numbness and dullness, turned, for in-
> stance, 'the curd-pale moon' into 'the brilliant moon', that all
> might seem, as it were, remembered with indifference, except
> some one vivid image.[6]

The revision to which Yeats refers was made about 1925
but the seed of the aesthetic theory upon which it was based
had been sown over fifty years before by his father, who told
his son that he "did not care even for a fine lyric passage unless
he felt some actual man behind its elaboration of beauty . . . "
(A, p. 65). The phrasing here is reminiscent of that in which
Yeats had praised poets like Villon for making the reader feel
"the presence of a man thinking and feeling," and the similarity
is perhaps more notable when we recall that this passage was

---

[6] A, pp. 263–264. The early poem from which Yeats quotes the
example is "The Sorrow of Love," first published in 1892 in *The
Countess Kathleen*. His memory goes slightly astray here in that the
word "crumbling" was substituted for "curd-pale" in the fourth stanza,
while "brilliant" was substituted for "full round" in the first stanza. The
import, however, is much the same.

extracted from a letter written *to* J.B. Yeats. The father's own early intuitions are coming back to him in his son's more refined formulation, and the image of a paternal influence as felicitous in its way as that of Leopold Mozart begins to crystallize when we read of J.B. Yeats' preference for poetry like that of Shakespeare, which embodies "An idealisation of speech," over the poetry of Keats, which he did not read, "caring little . . . for . . . poetry . . . from the influence of painting" (A, p. 65). Here, then, on a single page of the *Autobiographies* is the prototype of that dichotomy which opposed Keatsian "vision" to Shakespearean dramatic speech, and which was so central to Yeats' mature aesthetic.

Hence, I must disagree with Grossman when he finds Yeats' early development in lyric poetry to be a reaction against his father's ideals for that genre. Grossman gives a different interpretation to the passage above from "Reveries," seeing in J.B. Yeats' search for "the lineaments of some desirable familiar life" an aim at odds with the son's esoteric spiritualism; and in the song of the scornful spirits in *Manfred* the suggestion of a future Yeatsian style "which cannot 'even in anger put off its sweetness,'" and which the elder Yeats opposed. Prometheus, Coriolanus, and Manfred—the sort of "presences" whom J.B. Yeats admired—hardly represent the "familiar life" in any expected sense of that phrase, except so far as their respective crises are possible *human* crises in the face of overwhelming forces; and this is exactly the situation which the Yeatsian adept faces in *The Wind Among the Reeds*. And again, the word "sweetness" is hardly applicable in its usual sense to the tone of the spirits' utterances in Manfred—particularly in the case of the Seventh Spirit, whose scorn is quite equal to that of Prometheus at his most impassioned. The "familiar" and the "sweet" appear to have somewhat idiosyncratic meanings for J.B. Yeats, which preclude one taking them too literally; while "idealised speech" itself is a broad enough term to allow the degree of lyricism prevailing in the 1899 volume with which Grossman is mainly concerned. There is, admittedly, evidence to show that the father approved of the later poetry's turn toward less mystical dramatic situations; but there is no real basis for finding "rebellion" in the lyrical modes of the Eighties and Nineties, which represent after all (as will be seen) a coherent development toward the dramatization of the lyric. And this dramatization is, essentially, the core of J.B. Yeats' poetical ideal.

It was no doubt his father's predilection for "idealised speech" which led Yeats to begin his artistic career by writing poetic dramas, a practice in which he was encouraged by his fellow art student George Russell, who wrote similar pieces in competition.[7] *Mosada* and "Time and the Witch Vivien," both begun before Yeats's twentieth year, represent the sort of "passionate incidents" which he believed constituted the heart of Shakespeare's achievement. He later wrote in a letter to Frank Fay:

> I went to *The Merchant of Venice* the other night and . . . found that as usual for a Shakespearean play nothing moved me except scenes of prolonged crisis. The Trial scene was moving, but owing to the stage management the rest was broken up. Shakespeare had certainly intended these short scenes of his to be played one after the other as quickly as possible. (L, p. 465)

Certainly the emotional crises in *Mosada* come thick and fast: a magical ceremony taking place amid great tension is broken up by the arrival of "Officers of the Inquisition"; Ebremar, the chief inquisitor, unwittingly orders the execution of his old sweetheart Mosada: and finally Mosada swallows poison from a ring and dies for sixty lines of "prolonged crisis" in the arms of the horrified Ebremar. "Time and the Witch Vivien" is focused upon only one passionate encounter, between the beautiful heroine and the aged figure who comes to claim her, but the drama is lengthened by having Vivien play two consecutive games against her enemy—the first a throwing of dice for Time's hourglass, the second a chess game with "triumph" in the witch's "many plots." She loses both and dies.

[7] See Ellmann, *Masks*, p. 32.

The phrasings, cadences, and syntax of these and other early dramatic poems show just how strong an impression the language of Shakespeare made upon the early Yeats; the ghost of Richard II, for instance, "hammering out" his metaphysical conceits in the tower of Pomfret, broods over Vivien's stylized description of her fateful chess game:

> Thus play we first with pawns, poor things and weak;
> And then the great ones come, and last the king.
> So men in life and I in magic play;
> First dreams, and goblins, and the lesser sprites,
> And now with Father Time I'm face to face.

Another and more striking echo of Richard, this time in his "death of kings" speech before Barkloughly Castle (III. ii. 144–177), is heard in *The Island of Statues* when Naschina mournfully envisages the statue to be raised to her if she does not return:

> And once a-year let the Arcadians come,
> And 'neath it sit, and of the woven sum
> Of human sorrow let them moralize;
> And let them tell sad histories, till their eyes
> All swim with tears.
>
> (II. ii. 29–33)

In certain passages the attempt to produce casual banter between tragic moments is obviously Shakespearean in spirit: Vivien's flippant addressing of Time as "Old Father Wrinkles" and her pert dismissal of one of his replies with "Oh I am weary of that foolish tale" (l. 33) instance such attempts, in which the dangerous is braved with a certain nonchalance; while the light songs and comic utterances of the First Monk in *Mosada* have the same relation to imminent tragedy as does the "drunken porter" scene from *Macbeth*.

One senses here an ambition on Yeats' part to go beyond the "passionate incident" into the full Elizabethan variety and inspired heterogeneity of Shakespeare's plays; certainly this seems to be his aim in *The Island of Statues*, which prefaces its climactic third act with two lighter acts of a pastoral melange, including a comic singing match, fairy songs, the disguise of the heroine as a boy, and of course the woodland apparatus with which Yeats constructed his "region." The Shakespearean conception here is so basic that it seems to have escaped Yeats' notice when he was naming the influences of which he was conscious in the poem. An essay written in 1901 calls *The Island of Statues* a mixture of "Shelley and Spenser" whereas a much later one emphasizes the influence of *The Faerie Queene* and *The Sad Shepherd*.[8]

In these last two works we see the operation of those Elizabethan influences which encouraged the sense of "region" in Yeats' poetry rather than the sense of urgent speech, but provided him with examples of exotic characters in equally exotic situations. *The Sad Shepherd*, an unfinished play by Ben Jonson, furnished Yeats with a pastoral scene and the ominous presence of Maudlin, Witch of Papplewich, who has imprisoned the sweetheart of the shepherd Aeglamour in a tree. The analogy of this situation to that of pastoral Arcady, where an enchantress turns men to stone, is obvious and it is possible that Yeats found some prototype here. A more important similarity, perhaps, is in the respective characterizations of Aeglamour and Almintor, the former of whom is introduced by Jonson's prologue as the namesake of the play:

> . . . and in one Man
> As much of sadness showne, as Passion can.
> The sad young Shep'ard, whom wee here present,
> Like his woes Figure, darke and discontent,
> For his lost Love. . . .[9]

Aeglamour's sorrow is prompted by the frustration of his

[8] See, respectively, "What is 'Popular Poetry'?" E, p. 3, and "A General Introduction for my Work," E, p. 510.

[9] *The Sad Shepherd*, in *Ben Jonson*, ed. Herford and Simpson (Oxford, 1941), VII, "Prologue," ll. 19–23.

love, and so is that of Almintor, though in the latter case this frustration derives from the heroine's coolness and not from her physical imprisonment. What is notable is that Almintor indulges in an elaborate digression upon the basic sadness of nature as seen through his eyes, thus making his mood as predominant as that of Aeglamour:

> . . . look you, sad's the murmur of the bees,
> Yon wind goes sadly, and the grass and trees
> Reply like moaning of imprisoned elf:
> The whole world's sadly talking to itself.

(I. ii. 9–12)

Spenser's influence on *The Island of Statues* is more pervasive than that of Jonson, and is catalogued by Patty Gurd in her book on the early work of Yeats: the Italianate names, the island paradise, the contempt of the shepherdess for her unadventurous suitor, and various other details.[10] She does not seem to mention the singing match between Periglot and Willie in the "August Eclogue" of *The Shepheard's Calendar*, which is similar to that of Yeats' shepherds even in the alternation of voices in the same song. At the broadest level Yeats found warrant for the island's prolific and sometimes gratuitous natural beauties in Spenser, or perhaps one should say, in the Keatsian Spenser. Certainly it was a view of the Bower of Bliss as distinctly Romantic as the glorification of Milton's Satan which enabled Yeats to ignore Spenser's condemnation of sensuous beauty as an end in itself, and to write in his *Autobiographies*:

> In those islands [of Phaedria and Acrasia] certain qualities of beauty, certain forms of sensuous loveliness were separated from all the general purposes of life, as they had not been hitherto in European literature—and would not be again . . . till Keats wrote his *Endymion*. (p. 188)

---

[10] *The Early Poetry of William Butler Yeats* (Lancaster, Pa., 1916), pp. 21–23. Miss Gurd also gives an account of various specific influences of Shelley, with which I have not dealt here.

"Sensuous loveliness," however, suggests once again the cul-de-sac of descriptive poetry, and it is probable that, stylistically, Yeats found more in Spenser to hamper him than to help. He has a debt to Spenser for reinforcing a prototype of the isolated enchantress (which could be gleaned from more intensely dramatic sources in the Romantics, particularly Shelley). But it is to Shelley, Shakespeare, and Balzac that we must look for that portion of the early matrix which encouraged the growth of "dramatic speech" by helping to form the conception of personae exalted and intense enough to utter it.

What might be called the archetypal Yeatsian hero may be sensed in the various speeches of which J.B. Yeats approved—they all exhibit attitudes of scorn and defiance. The noble exile, even if his isolation is self-imposed, is hounded by impertinent commoners or by the powers of evil; and his reply, couched in haughty terms, suggests contempt for the worst that the enemy can do. Some magnificent gesture of independence and lofty indifference to the world gains by its very disregard for practical advantage an absolute value in terms of spiritual integrity.

Yeats, shy and awkward in argument as a young man, was immediately attracted to the "image of heroic self-possession" (A. p. 29) presented by Hamlet and others who possessed the ability "to play with hostile minds" (A. p. 57). A large part of the fascination lay in the transcendent ease with which the demands and accusations of the hostile were negated—an ease suggesting the facility of the master swordsman parrying almost nonchalantly the fierce attack of his opponents. Such a scene was that of Coriolanus in the house of Aufidius, which J.B. Yeats was fond of reading aloud:

> *3 Servingman.* Where dwell'st thou?
> *Coriolanus.* Under the canopy.
> *3 Servingman.* Under the canopy!
> *Coriolanus.* Ay.
> *3 Servingman.* Where's that?
> *Coriolanus.* I' the city of kites and crows.

> *3 Servingman.* I' the city of kites and crows!
>   What an ass it is! then thou dwell'st with daws too?
> *Coriolanus.* No, I serve not thy master.[11]
>
> (IV. v. 39–48)

It was this passage which floated into Yeats' mind when he first walked the lonely, impersonal streets of London "under the canopy . . . i' the city of kites and crows" (A. p. 95).

Shakespeare, as the *Autobiographies* indicated, was not the only repository of this attitude; it was evinced by a large number of Romantic heroes such as Byron's Manfred and Balzac's Lucien de Rubempré, in whom it achieved a certain purity by being freed from the humorous aura of verbal irony. More important to Yeats' own development, however, were the melancholy heroes of Shelley, who devoted enormous resources of intellect and spirit to solitary contemplation and the pursuit of the innermost secrets of nature. It was the mastery derived from arcane knowledge, and the tragic burdens borne in acquiring that knowledge which first fascinated Yeats—Alastor lingering among "ruined temples . . . and wild images / Of more than man" until he saw "The thrilling secrets of the birth of time"; Prince Athanase sequestered in his lonely tower with an aged tutor while the fisherman watched "their lamp from Laian's turret gleam, / Piercing the stormy darkness, like a star"; and Ahasuerus the Wandering Jew, master of all wisdom, living completely aloof from mankind in a "sea-cavern / Mid the Demonesi." [12] Both Bloom and George Bornstein deal with the important relationship between these personae and the Mask of Phase 17 as set forth in *A Vision*—the Mask of the naturally gregarious or dissolute lyric poet. It involves, says Yeats, "Simplification through intensity" and may "represent some intellectual or sexual passion; seem some Ahasuerus or Athanase; be the gaunt Dante of the *Divine Comedy*. . . . "

[11] *Coriolanus*, ed. J. Dover Wilson (Cambridge, 1960).
[12] See, respectively: *Alastor*, ll. 116–128; *Prince Athanase*, ll. 189–190. *Hellas*, ll. 163–164.

The sage-magician makes a definite appearance in Yeats' earliest poetry in the forms of Mosada, Vivien, and the fairy from *The Island of Statues*. Yeats's enchantresses were perhaps the last in a long line stretching from Homer's Circe down through Spenser's Acrasia and Phaedria, and Shelley's Witch of Atlas. Those of pre-Romantic vintage, such as "vyle" Acrasia, were usually cast in the role of antagonist, and used their arts and beauty to ensnare adventurers engaged in some worthy undertaking; their overthrow was simply the assertion of the poet's moral norm. With the rise of Romanticism, however, most such norms underwent considerable revision. The patina of forbidden glamor which has always surrounded the outlaw as a rejecter of conventional social values became the badge of a new brotherhood of the elect; and, since the practice of magic was an obvious means of accession to that unsocial vein of the daemonic in which the Romantic hero found at once his glory and his ruin, the sorceress took her place at least occasionally with the exile and the recluse as an example of spiritual integrity in a world of bourgeois compromise. Shelley's Witch of Atlas is a paragon of womanhood, dedicating her magical arts to the service of human happiness:

> A lovely lady garmented in light
>   From her own beauty—deep her eyes, as are
> Two openings of unfathomable night
>   Seen through a Temple's cloven roof—her hair
> Dark—the dim brain whirls dizzy with delight,
>   Picturing her form; her soft smiles shone afar,
> And her low voice was heard like love, and drew
> All living things towards this wonder new.
>   *The Witch of Atlas*, (ll. 81–88)

She became for Yeats the symbol of a transforming power, one of Shelley's "personifications of beauty," bringing reconciliation and honesty "when she moves over the enchanted river that is an image of all life . . ." (E. p. 68).

Yeats must have been the first, however, to elevate the enchantress to the position of tragic heroine. Both tragedy and physics share the maxim that the force of a fall depends partly upon the height previously achieved by the fallen, and the beautiful woman who has some measure of control over the elements obviously occupies a favored position. It was, after all, but a step from the mastery of human knowledge in a tower room to the study of inhuman arts—in both cases intercourse with society was rejected in favor of an attempt to metamorphose the self into a sort of demigod. That the years of dedication and solitude should at last bring nothing more than the common end of man was an outcome fraught with tragic implications for a young poet who himself entertained arcane ambitions, and he explores these implications as Mosada dies by poison in the Inquisitor's dungeon; as Vivien is checkmated by Time in a chess game on which her life is staked; and as the doomed Enchantress of *The Island of Statues* cries out to Naschina: "Oh death is horrible! and foul, foul, foul!" (II. iii. 238)

If we examine the description of the man of Phase 3—from which, according to Yeats, the lyric poet of Phase 17 obtains his Mask—we find that the enchantresses are not the only prototypes of the "anti-self" present in the early poetry:

> . . . (he) becomes an Image where simplicity and intensity are united, he seems to move among yellowing corn or underhanging grapes. He gave to Landor his shepherds and hamadryads, to Morris his *Waters of the Wondrous Isles*, to Shelley his wandering lovers and sages, and to Theocritus all his flocks and pastures. . . . (AV, p. 109)

Bloom, in reference to the same passage, asserts that "It is, of course, afterthought to find the *antithetical* quester in the shepherds, Indians, lovers, mad kings, fairies, fishermen, and fox-hunters of *Crossways*. . . ." But the afterthought sheds at least some light on the significance as "simplification" of the enchantresses, Arcadians, Anashuya and Vijaya, and the other pastoral inhabitants of Eastern paradises "where peahens dance, in crimson feather;" and also upon the relation between the failure of this dramatic technique and the early pictorial bias.

Shepherd and sage seem at first to be strange phase-fellows. It is easy to see simplicity in the former and intensity in the latter, but not the combination in both. Yeats describes the man of Phase 3 as being "Almost without intellect," and this would be a most peculiar characteristic to attribute to Ahasuerus or Athanase. The resolution lies partly in the simplification which the sage has achieved not only by retiring into solitude, but by successfully unravelling the mysteries of existence. His intellectual triumph no longer involves labor; it is complete, and represents the sort of calm, rich plenitude suggested by the "yellowing corn" and "overhanging grapes" in the landscape through which the shepherd moves, and by the shepherd's own "perfect bodily sanity." As for intensity, it is mainly the quality of the man of another phase who is striving for the simplicity which Phase 3 represents. By fierce desire and concentration he loses his equivocation, complexity, and incompleteness, and looks out through the eyes of lucid, harmonious fulfilment. In a sense, the intensity of an Ahasuerus or Athanase is not the property of this phase, but an antecedent condition resulting in an *achieved* wisdom which does belong.

This last point is important because it makes the sage-magician not merely a *primary* Mask, as the Indian is, but also a representative of Yeats himself as *antithetical* intensifier—especially in the case of the enchantresses, who can be seen, after all, as the ultimate in the lust for self-realization, the furthest from subservience to an inherited, objective order of things. To force nature into accord with one's subjective images is the final antithetical goal, and the enchantress' power becomes the literal realization, in myth, of the power which the poet of Phase 17 can exhibit only in an imaginative realm.

These considerations help to explain why the specific personae who represent Yeats' simplified "anti-self"—the enchantresses, and later the Fisherman, the Irish Airman, and the Berkeleyan poet—have Coriolanean qualities of noble independence and inviolate aloofness which are so well suited to dramatic exposition, but are seemingly at odds with the idyllic world of Phase 3. The overweening ego has "simplified" the confusing tangle of exterior reality, including conventional demands, into fodder for its own creative purposes. In Emily Dickinson's terms, one surrounds nature in a state of Circumference, rather than *being* surrounded in the fallen state of Centre. Or, to recall Yeats' praise of Shakespeare's characters (quoted above, p. 10) it is possible to imagine personae whose passion becomes "the whole energy of their being" and transforms objective nature into symbols and metaphors for the mind's convenience. But the dialectic between external reality and the individual psyche brings us back to the basic conflict of picture and drama in the early Yeats. The paradise of Phase 3, with its fecundity and abundance, is a *primary* world which invites acquiescence in the joy of nature's fullness, but not the transfiguration of nature to satisfy desires which would go beyond it; and it is just such a world which Yeats presents in the earliest poems. The heavy ripeness of Arcady mitigates the antithetical forcefulness of the enchantress' personality, and serves as a vivid but unconscious symbolization of her defeat, which is the defeat of dramatic subjectivity by objective physicality. I agree with Bloom in finding the defeat of the antithetical quester to be a Romantic legacy, but my point of divergence is that this legacy also involves a certain aesthetic failure. Alastor's and Endymion's psychic presences are diminished each time their creators yield to the urge to paint long, ecstatic portraits of the scenes which the heroes have visited, and it is only when Yeats yearns to escape this trap that he succeeds in communicating the *immediacy* of the antithetical personality more forcefully and dramatically than Keats or Shelley ever did.

In fairness to the Shelleyan influence, it must be pointed out that the diaphanous, Platonic imagery which it encouraged was congenial to the dramatization of antithetical man; it was merely the profusion and concentration of it in extended landscapes which interfered with the dramatic mode. Keats' imagery, on the other hand, with its color and earthly voluptuousness, was by its very nature inimical to that mode. As a result, although the paradises of both poets may be—as Bloom insists— "lower" paradises of blocked desire, the psychic energy of the blocked quester is much more evident in Shelley, whereas Keats envisages fulfilment so concretely that the imaginary nature of that fulfilment gives way to a sense of the tangible. Yeats' early paradises are Keatsian—even though they lack the energy of Keats' cornucopian rage—and thoroughly primary; and so are the Indian personae who inhabit them in a surfeit of contentment. Thus it is that the Indian does not suggest the antithetical desire which created him, and invites dismissal as a flaccid escapist whimsy. What Yeats had to discover was how to suggest the urgency and intensity of the man who was not fulfilled at the same time that he presented a vision of fulfilment which did not overwhelm this psychic immediacy with the concrete and uninvigorated world of subhuman nature.

The problem of enervation in the early paradises of Yeats leads us, however, to issues more basic than languorous scenery. The failure of the earliest poems to achieve dramatic impact, despite the dramaturgic bias of their author, goes beyond the intrusion of "picture" to the paradox of early Yeatsian "love," which is actually marked by an absence of wild emotion, and which represents a special case of the *fin-de-siècle* vitiation identified with Morris' *Earthly Paradise* and kindred works. There was a tendency among Neo-Romantics of the later nineteenth-century to read the letter rather than the spirit of Shelleyan and Keatsian law, robbing personae of the fierce, uncontrollable forces which had vitalized them and utilizing the colorful husks which remained. This tendency may be demonstrated in Yeats' early work by a comparison of Shelley's island paradise in *Epipsychidion* with the island which it obviously inspired in "The Indian to His Love." Shelley describes his refuge as:

> ... an isle twixt Heaven, Air, Earth, and Sea,
> Cradled, and hung in clear tranquillity;
> Bright as that wandering Eden Lucifer
> Washed by the soft blue Oceans of young air.
> It is a favoured place. Famine or Blight,
> Pestilence, War and Earthquake, never light
> Upon its mountain-peaks; blind vultures, they
> Sail onward far upon their fatal way:
> The winged storms, chanting their thunder-psalm
> To other lands, leave azure chasms of calm
> Over this isle, or weep themselves in dew,
> From which its fields and woods ever renew
> Their green and golden immortality . . . .

The complete description runs on for over one hundred fifty lines, and contains a great many images which must have appealed to the early Yeats: gentle pastoral folk; an atmosphere soporific with "the scent of lemon flowers"; and, of course, infinite harmony and "clear tranquillity."

There is a crucial difference, however, between the respective dramatizations of this tranquillity. Shelley's catalogue of the cosmic disasters from which the island is protected actually transfers a sort of negative energy to the island's bliss. The reader is given a vivid sense of the hostile maelstrom which seethes outside the paradise, so that the paradise itself, by resisting this hostility, acquires a reverse animation of its own. No such transferral occurs in the casual dismissal by Yeats' persona of "all earth's feverish lands"; we are left unconvinced of utopia as a *positive* escape.

One of the best cases in point is furnished by a comparison of the lovers' attitudes in the two poems. Shelley speaks of:

> One passion in twin-hearts which grows and grew,
> Till like two meteors of expanding flame. . . . (ll. 575–576)

The resemblance to Yeats' own lines in "The Indian to His Love" is too close for mere coincidence:

> While grows our love an Indian Star,
> A meteor of the burning heart. . . .

The poets, however, diverge revealingly in interpreting this meteoric love. Shelley makes it clear that his lovers will continue to enjoy the fervor of love, however symbolic its sexuality, as their lips "eclipse / The soul that burns between them;" but this fervor, with its implications of a raging Platonic energy, has been extracted from love in Yeats' island paradise, leaving only a simulacrum:

> . . . Love is kindly and deceitless
> And all is over save the murmur and sweetness.

The process of simplification here is perhaps more obvious than the intensity which has supposedly effected it. The Indian persona envisages a utopia in which tranquillity and languor are values so absolute that vigorous emotions have no place, and Yeats is faced with the paradox of a dramatic pose in which there are few of the passionate elements which make for drama.

This position was not entirely the result of inadvertent omission; it was in some measure due to Yeats' conscious desire, almost from the start, to invest his poetry with a certain coldness, the nature of which he at first misunderstood—it tended for some years to be the sort which turns things purple. He began by utilizing somewhat dampened and emasculated imagery and restricting himself to the treatment of a very narrow range of emotions centered around the sorrowful aftermath of tragedy. Even in *Mosada*, which is actually involved with the tragic crisis, the poet lingered almost interminably over the Moorish maiden's dying speech, indulging in such lines as:

> Poor love and sorrow, with their arms round
> Each other's necks, and whispering as they go,
> Still wander through the world. . . . (iii. 119–121)

In *The Island of Statues* and "Jealousy" we find even clearer examples of worlds in which sorrow never sinks to despair, and joy never rises to ebullience. All is in the middle register, and a minor key modulates in and out as various sorrows flit through the Arcadian and Indian paradises. Anashuya's song is illustrative:

> A sad, sad thought went by me slowly—
>
> . . . .
>
> The sad, sad thought has gone from me now wholly. . . .
> "Jealousy" (ll. 17–19)

Happiness, by the same token, seems to be as negative an affair as the old chestnut in which good was defined as the absence of evil.

Although real passion seldom entered such worlds, it bore a definite relation to them—a fact which further underlines Yeats's conscious awareness of some of the restrictions which he was imposing upon himself. In "Ephemera," for example, the melancholy mood which the poet was so fond of evoking is shown as the vitiated aftermath of the lovers' fervent emotion—"When the poor tired child passion falls asleep"—and the imagery of lame hares and autumn leaves is introduced in support of the mood. Similarly, the Indian persona implies recognition of an earlier time of tumult when he tells the woman that "All is over save the murmur and the sweetness."

We are faced here, however, with a knotty problem in artistic contrast. The enervation of the lovers in "Ephemera" is apparently intended as semi-tragic, while that of the pair in the Indian song is meant to be ultimately desirable. The first and unkindest temptation is to assume that the young Yeats and his aged muse were so taken with the possibilities of lifelessness that they tried to use it as an artistic catchall, but one is left with the suspicion that there is something more significant— although perhaps vaguely formulated—behind the poet's early strivings for "coldness." Consider, for instance, Yeats' essay on Spenser, written in 1902:

There is no passion in the pleasure he has set amid perilous seas for he would have us understand that there alone could the war-worn and the sea-worn man find dateless leisure and unrepining peace. (EI, p. 383)

Passion is here cast as something inimical to the calm of eternity, and as such must inevitably recall the "breathing human passion" which Keats opposed to the "cold pastoral" of the Grecian urn. It seems quite probable that Yeats, by making his Indian island passionless, sought also to make it timeless; the island is actually the prototype, however remote, of the supernatural states which he would later celebrate. By slowing the tempo of an imagined life through the removal of its tumult, and introducing static images like the parrot's reflection in "the dim enameled sea," Yeats was actually seeking a shortcut to the transcendent harmony of Byzantium. The fact that there was none—that the long road which led there from Arcady lay through the mire of humanity and not around it—does not obscure the fascination of seeing the impulse already active so early in the poet's career.

From the standpoint of the Romantic legacy, Yeats' earliest work may be said to suffer from an absence of the "apocalyptic vitalism" which Bloom rightly finds in the poet's great nineteenth-century predecessors; and in particular that form of "vitalism" which involves supernaturalism in its highest manifestation. In this form—which would soon distinguish *The Wind Among the Reeds*—perceived reality becomes a perpetual dialectic of the substantial everyday world and an active, intrusive realm of spirit, as in "Christabel" or the "stolen rowboat" scene of *The Prelude*. One encounters this form of supernaturalism, which we may term "the daemonic," [13] characteristically in Blake, Shelley, Coleridge, and Wordsworth, though Yeats was prevented from assimilating the direct influence of

[13] I am using this term in a sense which represents a slight modification of Plato's sense: "intermediate between god and mortal" (cited by Bornstein, p. xix).

this last poet by a distaste for the moralization which so frequently accompanied the descriptions of encounter with superhuman forces.[14] The energy deriving from treatments of the supernatural is not, of course, the only source of energy available to poets, and most get by quite well without it. But for Yeats—granted his orientation and his peculiar aesthetic psychology—it would always be most felicitous to look for subject matter at the juncture between a realm of concrete normality and an extraordinary realm of imagined powers and states of being, even though the latter would eventually change in contents from ghosts and the mystic Rose to realistic mental images. Without such a focus, in his earliest creative years, his art presented a deceptive smoothness of finish in which passion was not so much triumphantly contained as quietly eviscerated.

As the poet approached his twentieth year, however, the dam began to show signs of strain; increasing involvement in the activities of arcane societies brought into his life a new turbulence which was reflected in his art, and which marked the emergence of the daemonic strain. Looking back upon this period four years later, in 1888, Yeats wrote to Katherine Tynan:

> I was then living a quite harmonious poetic life. Never thinking out of my depth. Always harmonious, narrow, calm. Taking small interest in people but most ardently moved by the more minute kinds of natural beauty. 'Mosada' was then written and a poem called 'Time and Vivien' which you have not seen. . . . Everything done then was quite passionless. The 'Island [of Statues]' was the last. Since I have left the 'Island,' I have been going about on shoreless seas. Nothing anywhere has clear outline. Everything is cloud and foam. . . . The clouds began about four years ago. I was finishing the 'Island.' They came and robbed Naschina of her shadow. As you will see, the rest is cloudless, narrow and calm.[15]

[14] See, however, Bloom (Introduction) for a discussion of Wordsworth's indirect influence.

[15] L, p. 88. Actually, Yeats continued to indulge occasionally in "harmonious" compositions after 1885, if Ellmann is correct in assigning

Interest in this aesthetic revolution in Yeats' poetry has been pushed into the background by critical preoccupation with the later and more dramatic changes which took place, but there is little doubt that the appearance of the "cloud and foam" marked a new expansion of his metaphysic, as well as an attempt to come to grips with subject matter which demanded a more direct involvement and a more obvious intensity of expression than his earlier themes. The loss of Naschina's shadow, for instance, is perhaps more portentous than it at first appears.* A new dissonance sounds through the "harmonious" adventures in Arcadia when the Enchantress warns Naschina that her transformation into a fairy queen involves the payment of a terrible price:

> As an hurt leopard fills with ceaseless moan,
> And aimless wanderings the woodlands lone,
> Thy soul shall be, though pitiless and bright
> It is, yet shall it fail thee day and night
> Beneath the burthen of the infinite. . . . (II. iii. 208–212)

The conventional dangers of physical harm or death which had given point to deeds of bravery and defiance in earlier episodes have here given way to a supernatural peril which—if we disregard the frequent preciosity that emasculates the poem— is altogether more ominous in its implications of eternal alien-

---

"Anashuya and Vijaya" and "The Indian to his Love" to 1886 in *The Identity of Yeats* (London, 1954), p. 287. I have treated these Indian poems and the lyric "Remembrance" as members of the same early group as *Mosada*, *Vivien*, and *The Island of Statues* because they share an obvious community of spirit. Yeats seemed to give warrant for such a treatment when he wrote in a footnote to *Crossways* in 1895: "Many of these poems in *Crossways*, certainly those upon Indian subjects or upon shepherds and fauns, must have been written before I was twenty, for from the the moment when I began *The Wanderings of Oisin*, which I did at that age, I believe, my subject matter became Irish." (Quoted in the *Variorum Edition*, p. 841).

* *The Island of Statues* concludes with the stage direction: "The rising moon casts the shadows of Almintor and the Sleepers far across the grass. Close by Almintor's side, Naschina is standing shadowless."

ation from human destiny. Even the temporary victory over mortality is mitigated by the necessities of someday watching Almintor die, and of eventually feeling oneself fade into hopeless oblivion, as the song of the Voices points out:

> A man has a hope for heaven,
> But soulless a fairy dies,
> As a leaf that is old, and withered, and cold,
> When the wintry vapours rise. (II. iii. 248–251)

At first interested in arcane pursuits for their enhancement of the tragic isolation of his heroines, Yeats had come to see that the hunt for forbidden knowledge involved an interaction between the human and the superhuman which offered the possibilities for a drama of higher pitch and greater immediacy. Pastoral calm is violently shattered by supernatural horror in "The Seeker," first published in September, 1885. The forebodings which the shepherds feel despite their peace and prosperity are justified by the arrival of an aged knight, who insists upon visiting a nearby valley filled with unknown and inhuman terrors. Like the enchantresses, this knight-errant has a literary lineage stretching back to *The Odyssey*, but he is here etherealized as the typical Yeatsian dreamer who has wandered through places "Where spice-isles nestle on the star-trod seas" and has come at last to the forbidden valley, led on a quest beyond mortal understanding by mysterious voices. The "passionate incident" which climaxes the poem is the knight's encounter with the inspirer of his dreams, who turns out to be not a Beatrice-like image of divine beauty, but a grotesque witch personifying "Infamy."

Bloom interprets this ironic discovery as the natural result of a "lust after Infamy," presumably because the very nature of the knight's quest involves the reduction of a "man-of-action" to a "coward." This reading, however, does violence to the concept of elevation by superhuman love above the ignoble, "dreamless" remnant of his race which the knight clearly maintains. The infamy that he achieves was no more the object of his quest than the "infamy" which the hero of Joyce's "Araby" ironically achieves in his own eyes. An even more relevant parallel is found in Yeats' own poem "Fergus and the Druid," where the man-of-action who has turned away from the realm of action to the realm of dreams is surprised and devastated by the nature of his new "reward" of "wisdom." The purport of "The Seeker" is surely the daemonic purport of *The Island of Statues*: those who choose the *Hodos Chameliontos* over the conventional path risk spiritual destruction in their supernatural presumption.

Although Yeats considered "The Seeker" to be "readable" (L, p. 88), he left it out of the 1895 edition of the poems, along with the third scene of *The Island of Statues* and most of the other poems which reflected the period of turgidity through which he had passed. A vision of vast and ominous powers of infinite malevolence had encroached upon his neatly-fenced aesthetic, and he was as yet unable to control it. Years later he would find a comparable intrusion in Shelley's *Prometheus Unbound*.

> Demogorgon made his [Shelley's] plot incoherent, its interpretation impossible; it was thrust there by that something which again and again forced him to balance the object of desire conceived as miraculous and superhuman, with nightmare. (EI, p. 420)

Both Bornstein and Bloom find Yeats guilty here of a serious misinterpretation of Shelley; and the latter takes the passage as an example of the *clinamen*, or creative swerve away from the predecessor, which often characterizes Yeats' relation with Shelley. If there is such a swerve here, it reinforces the point I am making about Yeats' period of "cloud and foam," since the later poet would be distorting the earlier one's "problem" with Demogorgon into a semblable of his own aesthetic problem. At any rate, in Yeats' eyes Demogorgon became the prototype for the Shelleyan embodiment of evil, and as such begat a group of vague, titanic figures who hovered on the edge of nightmare:

> *Panthea.* What veiled form sits on that ebon throne?
> *Asia.* The veil has fallen.
> *Panthea.*   I see a mighty darkness
>   Filling the seat of power, and rays of gloom
>   Dart round, as light from the meridian sun.
>   —Ungazed upon and shapeless; neither limb,
>   Nor form, nor outline; yet we feel it is
>   A living Spirit.
>
> > *Prometheus Unbound*, (II. iv. 1–7)

"His political enemies," said Yeats of Shelley, "are monstrous, meaningless images" (AV, p. 143). These images seized the imagination of the Irish poet whose sense of political enmity was rapidly developing, and who was himself embarked upon an experiment in nightmare. In the poetry written between 1885 and 1888 there is a whole succession of supernatural antagonists inspired by Shelley's examples—Infamy, a darkened, enigmatic figure upon whom the light bursts to reveal a "bearded witch" with "dull unmoving eyes"; the allegorical representation of the English oppressor in "The Two Titans," with "fierce face as of a hound" and "spotted flesh and flying hair / And . . . gigantic limbs"; and finally Oisin's formless opponent, "A dusk demon, dry as a withered sedge," who changes progressively to a fir tree and the corpse of a drowned man.

Yet another group of massive, darkly-realized figures lack the quality of malignant deformity associated with witches and demons, but are imagined on an equally superhuman and awe-inspiring scale. They exhibit in various degrees a titanic lethargy which seems to be the ultimate intensification of early Yeatsian languor, and which ranges from the chain-hampered movements of the Irish titan to the absolute immobility of enormous statues. Both scale and attitude derive from the Romantics' grandiose treatments of mythology. Behind the long-suffering "grey-haired youth" of "The Two Titans," chained to his aggressive English enemy, lurks not only Shelley's Prometheus, bound to a rock at the mercy of the Furies, but the Glaucus of Keats's *Endymion*, whose rock of imprisonment—like that of Yeats' poem—is surrounded by the sea.[16]

In the third book of "The Wanderings of Oisin" the hero comes upon a "monstrous slumbering folk, / Their mighty and naked and gleaming bodies heaped loose where they lay" (ll. 27–28). Here the most obvious Romantic prototype is found in the opening scene of *Hyperion*, where the "frozen God" Saturn is seen sleeping "Like natural sculpture in cathedral cavern" (l. 86). A striking resemblance between Oisin's description of the Sleepers and the passage in "Anashuya and Vijaya" on "the parents of gods" underlines the fact that the image was one which haunted Yeats during this period:

> *Anashuya.* Swear by the parents of the gods,
>   Dread oath, who dwell on sacred Himalay—
>   On the far Golden Peak—enormous shapes,
>   Who still were old when the great sea was young;
>   On their vast faces mystery and dreams;
>   Their hair along the mountains rolled and filled
>   From year to year by the unnumbered nests
>   Of aweless birds, and round their stirless feet
>   The joyous flocks of deer and antelopes,
>   Who never heard the unforgiving hound. (ll. 66–75)

Although the titans of Anashuya are not described as "slumbering," they do have "stirless feet" and the sort of hair described in the Sleepers by Oisin: "the owls had builded their nests in their locks"—a somewhat unnerving detail designed to enforce the impression of long immobility. All their faces reflect an eternity of dreaming and in "Oisin" the impression of an im-

[16] See Bloom, p. 55, for a detailed commentary on the Shelleyan background of "The Two Titans." Bloom asserts that Yeats has "misleadingly" subtitled the work "A Political Poem," thus causing Ellmann (q.v. *Masks*, 48–9) to read it "reductively." But the subtitle makes it quite clear that Ellmann has fathomed Yeats' intentions on at least the first symbolic level.

mense weariness is emphasized, as though Yeats sought to present the apotheosis of a withering into truth.

Once again, as in the case of the cold paradise, we must question whether we are faced with an immature and temporary predilection for a particular complex of emotions and images, or with an early and vaguely realized manifestation of the author's mature aesthetic; and again, the evidence favors the latter possibility. An implication of the significance which this phantasmagoria of gigantic forms possessed for Yeats is found in his essay "The Tragic Theatre," written over thirty years after he had begun "The Wanderings of Oisin":

> . . . in mainly tragic art one distinguishes devices to exclude or lessen character, to diminish the power of that daily mood, to cheat or blind its too clear perception. If the real world is not altogether rejected, it is but touched here and there, and into the places we have left empty we summon rhythm, balance, pattern, images that remind us of vast passions, the vagueness of past times, all the chimeras that haunt the edge of trance. (EI, p. 243)

The poet would not have been able to state his aims so clearly in 1885, but it appears that he was already groping in his art toward a rejection of the ephemeral and accidental in favor of some comprehensive embodiment of passion at its most universal; toward the pure tragic vision, free of the limitations imposed by human nature in man's less exalted moods. "Vast passions" could most readily be exhibited in vast figures like the titans and the Sleepers that transcended altogether the idiosyncrasies of "character," staring out of impersonal faces whose inscrutability is broken only by the passive sorrow of solitary contemplation; while the "chimeras" from "the edge of trance" were crudely foreshadowed by the witches and demons—the nightmarish antagonists derived from Demogorgon.

In "Estrangement" Yeats delineated his conception of "the masks of tragedy":

The masks of tragedy contain neither character nor personal

energy. They are allied to decoration and to the abstract figures of Egyptian temples. Before the mind can look out their eyes the active will perishes, hence their sorrowful calm. (A, p. 286)

Egyptian artifice here furnishes Yeats with the ultimate example of the remote and impassive tragic attitude; the coldness of painted stone can never quite be attained by man, since some portion of active will is intrinsic to human life. The equivalent of these "abstract figures" in the early poetry is provided by statuary, which fascinated the poet by its massive, silent presence. In the first act of *The Island of Statues*, the figures of those who have been turned into stone merely lend an air of the magical and exotic and are characterized by Almintor in terms carefully selected to avoid disturbing the atmosphere of serenity:

> . . . Statue! O, thou
> Whose beard a moonlight river is, whose brow
> Is stone: old sleeper! (I. iii. 72–74)

However, by the time of "The Wanderings of Oisin," the statues had taken their place in the menagerie of terror, and the possibilities which they offered as brooding, ominous auguries of some supernatural experience were realized in Book II where Oisin enters the castle on the Isle of Victories:

> . . . Sat either side,
> Fog-dripping, pedestalled above the tide,
> Huge forms of stone; between the lids of one
> The imaged meteors had shone and run,
> And had disported in the eyes still jet
> For centuries, and stars had dawned and set.
> He seemed the watcher for a sign. (ll. 35–41)

As the antipodes of tragic passion and character became clearer in Yeats' mind, the statues took on far more refined and specific connotations as a mask for the former;* I am concerned at this point only with the emergence of the image, along with

* See Chap. V, p. 165.

that of the sleeping titans, in attitudes and contexts which connote the superhuman scale of the arena in which the poet sensed that that mask must operate—the scale implied by the statues' precedence over such elemental phenomena as "Time and Death and Sleep" in an 1895 emendation to the passage quoted above from "The Wanderings of Oisin." Even though he did not yet understand the mechanism of tragedy, Yeats had had an intuition of the vast cosmic repercussions and ramifications which its attitudes involved. The looming, immobile statues and sleeping demigods represent an attempt, however premature, to suggest this universality.

The period of "cloud and foam" brought with it not only unwieldy images of the daemonic but new and precarious experiments in form. Yeats had not resolved the antimony of dramatic attitude and description in earlier poems, but he had at least managed to establish setting and sequence of events with some degree of smoothness through the explanations embedded in the speeches of the various *dramatis personae*. Neither was any problem raised by the songs interspersed through the scenes, for these required little more than the evocation of some variety of sorrow. When Yeats sought, however, to incorporate a strong element of third person narrative in short non-dramatic poems, he encountered unexpected difficulties. Unable to borrow overtones or background from a dramatic context, he was faced with a poetical *tabula rasa* on which it was necessary to create the picture of an occurrence even as one sought to indicate the emotional intensity and spiritual significance which the occurrence possessed.

This, of course, is one of the basic problems of all short poems which are based upon particular occasions, and most successful poets arrive at some organic combination of event and significance. For Yeats, however, the problem was complicated by an imagination which had been taught to see all in terms of drama; his temporary solution was to open the poem with a description of characters and scene reminiscent of a

playwright's stage directions. This approach not only gave the
opening an aura of stiffness and artificiality; it also increased
the static painter's quality which Yeats was already trying to
overcome. "The Two Titans" opens with such a setting:

> The vision of a rock where lightnings whirl'd
> Bruising the darkness with their crackling light;
> The waves, enormous wanderers of the world,
> Beat on it with their hammers day and night.
> Two figures crouching on the black rock, bound
> To one another with a coiling chain. . . .

and in "How Ferencz Renyi Kept Silent," the protagonists are
carefully placed in position:

> Before his tent the General sips his wine,
> Waves off the flies, and warms him in the shine.
> The Austrian Haynau he, in many lands
> Famous, a man of rules, a victor. Stands
> Before him one well guarded, with bound hands;
> Schoolmaster he, a dreamer, fiddler, first
> In every dance, by children sought. . . . (ll. 6–12)

This poem also illustrates the closely-related problem of narrative continuity which beset Yeats at this time. He knew the
significant stages of his story but seemed uncertain how to
achieve a smooth transition between them; as a result the plot
unfolded in sporadic bursts which sometimes gave an effect of
absurd simplicity:

> To his hands she clings,
> With cries and murmurs. Suddenly he flings
> Away her clinging hands, and turns. She throws
> Her arms around his feet. The signal goes
> From Haynau's lifted fingers. . . .

A similar problem is evident in "She Dwelt Among the Sycamores" where Yeats devotes his first stanza to "A little boy
outside the sycamore wood" and then jumps suddenly in the
fifth line to "A little boy inside the sycamore wood."

The sense of uneven progress is sometimes deepened by one of Yeats' early attempts to achieve what he later called "a powerful and passionate syntax" (EI, pp. 521–522). Narrative of moments of emotional crisis called for a new voice on the part of the poet, who had to convey the dramatic tension of these moments without speaking in *dramatis persona*. Granted license, perhaps, by the "cloud and foam," Yeats began to experiment with disturbances of normal syntax such as ellipses, unusual inversions, and the sort of staccato sentences quoted above in the examples from "Ferencz Renyi." It was as though an attempt were being made to translate the abruptness and compression of these syntactical patterns directly into emotional equivalents which would heighten the tension, immediacy, and decisiveness of the unfolding drama. Verbs are left out of descriptions in order to make them terser, transitional phrases are ignored or weakened so as to be less evident, and modifying phrases are moved freely about.

The concatenation of these effects is found in "Ferencz Renyi" and to a lesser extent in "The Two Titans," both of which are highly experimental; but one inversion, in which the verb is placed at the beginning of independent clauses, seems to have exerted a particular and slightly more lasting attraction for Yeats. In "The Phantom Ship," for instance, published in 1888, we find:

> Prayed those forgotten fishers, till in the eastern skies
> Came olive fires of Morning and on the darkness fled,
> By the slow heaving ocean—mumbling mother of the dead.

The last and most important occurrence of this pattern is in the second book of "The Wanderings of Oisin," where it furnishes a characteristic element in the heroic meter of the "Isle of Victories" episode. As such, however, it is bound up with the influence of Sir Samuel Ferguson, and is better examined in relation to Yeats' attempt to discover a style congruous with the material of the Irish epic.

II

Patriotism Versus Art:
The Irish Background

ONE HAS ONLY TO EXAMINE THE POLITICAL IM-
plications of "Ferencz Renyi" and "The Two Titans" in order
to see that Yeats's nascent nationalism was reflected in his verse
by more than a vague turbulence; the artistic matrix, previously
characterized by the cosmopolitanism of the Elizabethans and
Romantics, began to take on a specifically Irish coloring in the
later years of the Eighties. In general, the intrusion of Irish
supernaturalism tended to strengthen that portion of the Romantic heritage which centered upon the daemonic by provid-
ing Yeats with a new cast of superhuman personae and a rich
tradition of encounter between these personae and man, though
the triviality of the "fairy" ballads temporarily weakened the
power of this daemonic strain. On the other hand, Yeats became deeply dissatisfied with the foreign exoticism of Romantic imagery; the discovery that his verses were "too full of the
reds and yellows Shelley gathered in Italy" led him to consider
"sleeping upon a board" in order to inculcate them with the
desired coldness (EI, p. 5).

Fortunately, a less violent escape from rootless flamboyance
was suggested by the influence of John O'Leary and other Irish
nationalists, who set Yeats to dreaming of a great national liter-

ature which would embody the essence of the historical Irish spirit in native images and myths, and would join peasant to aristocrat in a single, sweeping vision of cultural autonomy. Yeats, to be sure, somewhat exaggerated O'Leary's role in his development when he asserted in the *Autobiographies*: "From these debates [of the Young Ireland Society], from O'Leary's conversation, and from the Irish books he lent or gave me has come all I have set my hand to since" (p. 62). What is certain is that the aged Fenian statesman infused the young poet with the sort of nationalism too lofty to stoop or "oratorical or insincere verse" for its expression, and exposed him to the more worthy portion of the Irish literary heritage by lending him the poems of Mangan and Ferguson.

Vivid evidence of the dangers attendant upon the poet's immersion in a patriotic atmosphere was provided by the bombastic and sentimental rhetoric of the poetry produced by Yeats' fellow Young Irelanders. These writers—who included Katherine Tynan, T. W. Rolleston, Ellen O'Leary, Douglas Hyde, and others—were following a tradition of nationalistic verse which had begun to flourish with the founding of the Young Ireland Party in 1842. Made up of young men who wrote for the *Nation* newspaper, the original group had combined fiery polemics against the English oppressors with unabashed eulogy of Ireland and everything Irish. Edmund Curtis described them as being:

> . . . full of the romantic liberalism of the time which animated men like Garibaldi and Kosciusko. . . . To a large extent it was a revival of the Gaelic, militant, and aristocratic spirit, and the cult of 'The Dark Rosaleen'. . . spreading among the common people.[1]

Their spearhead was Thomas Davis, whose high purpose and fervor were admirable in themselves, but proved grave liabilities when they were brought to bear upon the writing of verses

[1] *A History of Ireland*, 6th ed., revised (London, 1950), pp. 366–367.

artless and openly emotional to the point of embarrassment. Nonetheless, patriotism being what it is, he was accorded great prominence as a poet by succeeding generations of Irishmen, and his untimely death at the age of thirty-one transformed him into a symbol of the blighted promise of Ireland herself.

The legacy of Davis and the other *Nation* writers is all too evident in a volume of poetry published in 1888 and entitled *Poems and Ballads of Young Ireland*. Technique, which was already costing Yeats great pains, is taken for granted; it is the thought that counts. Facile personifications in which Ireland is cast as a talking landscape or as a mother who would gladly press the careworn exile to her bosom alternate with nostalgic descriptions of Irish topography, and dramatic monologues in which the exiles themselves lament their absence in hackneyed and blatantly sentimental terms:

> In this far-off country, this city dreary,
> I languished weary, and sad, and sore,
> Till the flower of youth in glooms o'ershaded
> Grew seared, and faded for evermore.[2]

The old dichotomy of villainous England and virtuous, persecuted Ireland inevitably emerges, taking a somewhat extreme form in "A Ballad of '98," where the Irish partisan watches gleefully as a troop of English cavalry plunge over a cliff to their deaths. Not even love poetry was safe from creeping didacticism; Katherine Tynan's "Papist and Puritan" celebrates a marriage in which Catholic regality and Cromwellian fortitude combine to create the indomitable spirit of Ireland. Such verses furnished the grounds for Yeats' bitter complaint in "Ireland after Parnell":

> If one examined some country love-song, one discovered that it was not written by a man in love, but by a patriot who wanted to prove that we did indeed possess, in the words of Daniel O'Connell, 'the finest peasantry upon earth.' (A, p. 124)

[2] (Dublin). The quotation is from An Chraoibhin Aoibhinn's "Death Lament of John O'Mahoney."

There was, however, another tradition of Irish poetry which found its roots in the earliest stages of the country's history, and which offered Yeats an alternative to the empty rhetoric and homiletic intent of the Davis school. It was represented by the surviving fragments of ancient Gaelic poetry; by the adaptations from Irish myth of poets like Edward Walsh, James Mangan, and Sir Samuel Ferguson; and by modern attempts to write songs and epic poetry in Gaelic, such as the eighteenth-century version of Oisin's wanderings which furnished Yeats with a source for his poem. William Allingham should also be included with this group since his poems, although not modelled upon Celtic originals, were largely treatments of indigenous Irish folklore.

Grossman offers a somewhat different analysis of the Irish alternatives available to Yeats in his early years (*Poetic Knowledge in the Early Yeats*, pp. 5–6):

> Within the general field of Irish national literature in the nineteenth century at least two basic styles must be distinguished. The first is the purely national style allied to the rhetoric of '48, to the poetry of Samuel Ferguson, who is the literary representative of the later Fenian movement, and to Irish colloquial poetry. It continued to be written in both Ireland and England throughout the nineties and is associated with Catholicism and the less exacting, parochial audience of Catholic nationalism. The second is the literature of Celticism, which was almost entirely a product of Yeats' mind and was intimately associated with the development of post-Romantic literature in England and on the continent.

It is true that the work of Ferguson and Allingham does not belong to the "European tradition of occult wisdom" for which Grossman reserves his "Celtic" category; but neither do they belong in certain crucial respects with the "rhetoric of '48." They represent, as I hope to show, a differentiable element within the Nationalistic movement—an element more complexly related to the main line of Yeats's development in the Nineties than Grossman's categories imply.

At its best the older-Celtic variety of poetry offered a diction characterized by simplicity, poignance, dignity, and an imagery suggestive of the kinship which man alternately enjoyed and endured with the wilder elements of nature before bourgeois society isolated him from them. Time and again there is a quaint turn of thought upon some theme of love or war which, however formulaic it may have been for the early Gaelic poets, gives the impression of a fresh encounter with the eternal human crises. Such is the verse from the Aran Islands song which Yeats quotes at length in an essay:

> It is late last night the dog was speaking of you; the snipe was speaking of you in her deep marsh. It is you are the lonely bird throughout the woods; and that you may be without a mate until you find me. (EI, p. 9)

In those poems which actually treated subjects from the legends or mythologies of Ireland, concentration upon the story line provided an extra dimension of artistic distancing lacking in the raw outcries of pathos and moralization so frequently characteristic of Young Ireland nationalists. This group had unfortunately managed to get around the objectivity of narrative form by choosing openly patriotic plots, or by tacking a moral onto an old anecdote, as Chraoibhin had done when he closed the story of St. Colum-cille and the heron with the lines:

> So Colum, feeling though far away,
> For Ireland's soil—like the Gael to-day—
> Won favour in Heaven's sight.

An illuminating contrast between the rhetorical poetry of the Davis school and the colder, Gaelic-inspired poetry may be observed in the very Young Ireland volume of 1888 from which the unhappy examples quoted above were taken; indeed, the contrast is sometimes found within the work of a single poet. An Chraoibhin Aoibhinn, for example, was actually Douglas Hyde, an outstanding Gaelic scholar who was capable of translating fragments like that entitled "From the Irish" with felicitous results. The felicity is especially apparent when we compare his treatment of the older poetry with the patriotic vacuity of his own "Marching Song of the Gaelic Athletes," which precedes the Irish fragment in the volume. Even more revealing is the antithesis provided by T. W. Rolleston's "Song of the Wicklow Seas," on the one hand, and his rendering of "The Dead at Clonmacnoise" on the other. The former work is a pallid reflection of Wordsworth, with its catalogue of rewarding natural vistas and its closing invocation to the "bays of Wicklow":

> Waves, wash my spirit! and lonely places,
> If well I loved you, and aught you know,
> Make pure my life with immortal traces
> Of something in me that tells of you!

The latter, however, subtitled "From the Irish of Enoch O'Gillian," catches something of the lofty and beautifully controlled sadness of the aftermath of epic tragedy:

> Many and many a son of Conn the Hundred-Fighter
> In the red earth lies at rest;
> Many a blue eye of Clan Colman the turf covers,
> Many a swan-white breast.

Coming upon these Celtic poems in the Young Ireland collection is like standing before an open window in a stale Victorian attic, despite one's consciousness that the writers look backward to proven techniques and subjects of antiquity rather than directly encountering the problem of responding to contemporary situations. Yeats put his finger upon the reason for Young Ireland's failure to solve this problem when he contrasted the "newspaper rhetoric" of Thomas Davis with the language of Elizabethan times, when a man who was moved "could not but speak nobly":

> Men of the camp and of the council board, like Raleigh and Sydney, could not but be great poets, but when the language

is worn down to mere abstraction by a perpetual mechanical use, nobody can write tolerably, unless by some momentary accident without exhausting continuous sedentary labour.[3]

Yeats does not, perhaps, make allowance here for man's ingenuity in expressing himself vulgarly no matter what his milieu, but his central point is neatly demonstrated by the refreshing wind which blows through the verses of Rolleston and the others when they adopt a style which owes more to the childhood of the race than it does to the tired aesthetic of contemporary journalism.

The *Essays* and *Autobiographies* contain a myriad of references to the artistic difficulties raised by Irish nationalism, and in almost every case Yeats shows himself painfully aware of the gap between the literary distinction inherent in the ancient Gaelic tradition and the distorted representation which the true Irish spirit had received in the Young Ireland verse of "moral purpose and educational fervor" derived stylistically from "Campbell, Scott, Macaulay, and Beranger" (A, p. 123). In his essay "What is 'Popular Poetry'?" he includes the names of Longfellow, Mrs. Hemans, and Scott in a similar list, and emphasizes that the sort of "popular poetry" which these writers have produced belongs not to the imaginative peasantry but to the middle class, who represent an unfortunate halfway-house between the cultured appreciators of *Epipsychidion* and the completely "unlettered" folk bound by "unwritten tradition ... to the beginning of time and to the foundation of the world" (EI, p. 6).

It is somewhat surprising to learn that the Yeats who was so dedicated to the perpetuation of arcane mysteries and esoteric brotherhoods could express at one stage of his career a distaste for the literature of the "coteries" and could consciously seek to write in a "popular" vein which would "please everybody." He quickly discovered, of course, that he was misjudging the nature and audience of popular poetry, and arrived at a new

[3] Yeats, *Tribute to Thomas Davis* (Oxford, 1947), pp. 14–15.

viewpoint which made coteries and peasantry sharers of a common artistic speech which "delighted in rhythmical animation, in idiom, in images, in words full of far-off suggestion" (EI, p. 11), while the melodramatic poetry of the bourgeoisie was relegated to the lower circles of aesthetic hell.

This relegation, however, was perhaps not quite so simple and clearcut as it appears in the essay. Yeats retained his idealistic dream of a literature which would unite Ireland in a vision of its spiritual magnificence, however dormant this magnificence might be, and he was not without sympathy for the efforts of Davis and his successors to reach a large audience with a message of the nation's tragic stature and inherent virtues. Although he never really compromised the integrity of his own verse, he reviewed some of the more flatulent productions of the Young Ireland poets with a generosity and forbearance which obscured their essential mediocrity. One has only to open the pages of *Letters to the New Island* to find paragraph after paragraph of half-hearted encomium for authors who sank almost immediately into limbo.

Yeats was motivated not only by a desire to fan the newly kindled flame of a national literature, but by a genuine respect for the apparent sincerity of patriotic emotion which moved him even in poetry full of the most conventional rhetoric. He describes in "Reveries" how his eyes filled with tears upon reading a verse description of Ireland as seen by a "returning dying emigrant" despite the "vague, abstract words such as one finds in a newspaper." Impressed by the fact that the verses contained "the actual thoughts of a man at a passionate moment of life," Yeats began to suspect that "personal utterance . . . could be as fine an escape from rhetoric and abstraction as drama itself" (A, p. 63). The connection with the letter written years later to J.B. Yeats, in which the poet expressed his desire to give the impression of a "man thinking and feeling" * is obvious, and it becomes apparent that Young Ireland poetry, for all its rhetori-

* See above, Chap. I, p. 13.

cal defects, played some part in encouraging Yeats to develop
that mode of dramatic personal speech which he would utilize
in most of his greater poems.

Although it was J.B. Yeats who had first developed in his son
a predilection for the forcefulness of dramatic dialogue and
soliloquy as opposed to the more passive speech usually identified with the lyric, the father immediately objected to the attempt to make "personal utterance" a valid mode of poetical
expression, insisting that it "was only egotism" (A, p. 63). Both
men were right in their respective ways, and it was greatly to
Yeats' credit that he eventually arrived at a synthesis of the two
views which made it possible to lend the lyric the desired immediacy by making it dependent upon a dramatic pose which was
itself too objective and too removed from the rawness of actual
life to seem egotistical. Paradoxically, it was necessary to grow
impersonal and inactive in "sedentary toil" before one could
give the poetical impression of an active man in vital relation to
the flow of life about him. Otherwise, when one attempted to
move directly from the immediacy of life to the immediacy of
verse, as Davis and his followers had done, the result was "the
struggle of the fly in marmalade." [4]

Even as early as 1888 Yeats was exhibiting his ability to establish a positive and beneficial relationship to the Irish tradition
in at least two ways: by endowing the persona of the popular
dramatic monologue with a strong aura of independent presence, as opposed to the aura of raw self-exposure in the monologues of his Irish contemporaries; and by attaching himself to
the "ancient Irish portion of the tradition." His "King Goll,"
far and away the finest performance in the Young Ireland
volume, demonstrates not only a coherent pose but a use of
Irish materials far more promising than that represented by
sentimental chauvinism. Celtic mythology is the vehicle for a
mental drama which is not tinged with didactic overtones, but
is an aesthetic end in itself. Although the poem is almost com-

[4] Yeats, "Ego Dominus Tuus."

pletely Irish in setting and imagery, its effectiveness rests upon a study of human experience both of political enmities and of a patriotic *donneé* unacceptable to those of other nations.

Yeats' superiority in the monologue form is immediately apparent when we juxtapose a poem like Hyde's "Death Lament of John O'Mahoney" with "King Goll." One of the terms which Yeats most often applied to conventionally rhetorical poetry such as that of Young Ireland was "abstract," and the word's pejorative connotations become clear in connection with Hyde's poem. The persona O'Mahoney, exiled in America and dying, tells *about* his fate in diction which has the emotional neutrality identified with treatises on moral philosophy and the earnest exhortations of high school valedictorians. It is as though he were reviewing his life in terms of categories such as "contriving, hoping, striving" rather than in terms of vivid confrontations, conflicts, and states of mind which appeal directly to the aesthetic perceptions:

> In a foreign land, in a lonesome city,
>   With few to pity, or know, or care,
> I sleep each night while my heart is burning
>   And wake each morning to new despair.

Yeats, however, avoids the danger of circumventing these perceptions by actually dramatizing his royal persona through concentration upon significant actions and reactions and upon the poetical ramifications of the persona's madness—a madness enhanced by the suggestion of mystical insight which accompanies it, as Goll tells of hearing ". . . on hill heads high / A tramping of tremendous feet." The gestures and attitudes which Goll assumes are presented as though with an eye to their stage effect, and the poet is careful to provide him with the proper suggestion of background as he descends from throne to wilderness. Yeats' effective use of posture and of action, both mental and physical, is evident in stanza three, where madness comes upon the king in the midst of battle:

But slowly as I shouting slew
   And trampled in the bubbling mire,
In my most secret spirit grew
   A fever and a whirling fire.
I paused—the stars above me shone
   And shone around the eyes of men;
I paused—and far away rushed on
   Over the heath and spungy fen
And crumpled in my hands the staff
Of my long spear, with scream and laugh
And song that down the valley rolled—
(They will not hush, the leaves a-flutter round—
   the beech leaves old).

Some other Young Ireland poets aspired to construct dramatic monologues based upon legendary Gaelic personae, but the results—though happier than in Hyde's "Lament"—do not really merit comparison with those achieved by Yeats, who had obviously found his métier. Charles Fagan, for example, treats the ancient theme of the father unknowingly killing his son in combat, but the opening of "The Story of Clessamnor" is rather trite:

Friends, I am wounded in the fight:
I shall be dead ere fall the night . . . .

These lines set the tone for a series of monotonous couplets which one feels, somehow, could not possibly have followed from Yeats' impressive plunge *in mediā personā*:

Mine was a chair of skins and gold,
   Wolf-breeding mountains, galleried Eman. . . .

Yeats' progress in making his poetry Celtic is also evident in "King Goll," despite a lingering fondness for "leopard-coloured trees." Yeats achieves here, perhaps for the first time, the ambition of making his verses "hold, as in a mirror, the colours of one's own climate and scenery in their right proportion. . . ." (EI, p. 5). The mention of wolves and salmon indicates a conscious effort to capture the flavor of early Celtic nature poetry, which contained extensive catalogues of native flora and fauna, while the choice of the "King Goll" myth linked Yeats' work with the oldest Gaelic tradition. The theme of the solitary lamenting his former condition of wealth and happiness is common to the origins of all Northern poetry; one of the more familiar Anglo-Saxon examples is "The Wanderer," in which a lonely warrior mourns his perpetual exile from kinsmen and mead hall. External nature enters this lyric as one of the ubiquitous enemies of man, heightening the trenchancy of the elegiac mood.

In old Gaelic literature a well-defined group of these elegies is centered upon a figure whom Kenneth Jackson calls "The Wild Man of the Woods." [5] Unlike his Anglo-Saxon cousins, the Wild Man has been driven mad in a battle and has fled into the woods where, according to Jackson, "He wavers between despair at his dismal surroundings and joy in their beauty." This alternation of moods is far more marked than it ever is in Anglo-Saxon lyrics, in which a tone of sadness invades even the moment of joy at the sound of the cuckoo's voice heralding spring. Thus it is that Yeats' Goll wanders not only "along the wintry strands" but among images of plentitude "in the woods, / When summer gluts the golden bees."

In a subgroup of the "Wild Man" elegies from the twelfth-century Buile Shuibhe, the protagonist is Suibhe Geilt, the king of Dal Araide, and it is obvious that such poems are prototypes for Yeats' treatment of a mad king. One of the few surviving poems of this subgroup is of particular interest:

> Aspen a-trembling,
> at times when I hear
> its leaves rustling
> I think it is the foray. (Jackson, XI, 12)

The noise of the leaves' movement as a correlative for the an-

[5] *Studies in Early Celtic Nature Poetry* (Cambridge, 1935), p. 111.

guished, mysterious machinations of a disturbed mind is re-
peated in the refrain which Yeats affixes to each stanza of his
own poem—"They will not hush, the leaves a-flutter round
me—the beech leaves old"—and indicates the extent to which
he had attempted to root his own work in the very foundations
of the Irish imagination.

By the time of "King Goll" Yeats has discovered how nationalism might inform art without dominating it, but we may
look back two years to a brief interval of doubt in which two
attempts at patriotic verse hovered dangerously close to aesthetic compromise in the manner of Davis and company. "The Two
Titans" and "How Ferencz Renyi Kept Silent" represented experiments not only in syntax, narrative form, and imagery, but
in the relation of poetry to political sympathies. Since Yeats
possessed what seems to have been a constitutional aversion to
mere rhymed rhetoric, he was faced with the problem of finding a form which would give palatable artistic shape to sentiments which he must have instinctively realized were not the
stuff of poetry. One obvious—indeed, too obvious—solution was
suggested by the allegorical mode of Shelley's *Prometheus Unbound*, which provides the archetype for "The Two Titans."
Yeats did not go so far as to equate his hero with mankind's un-
quenchable desire for freedom, but he left no doubt that his two
gigantic, shadowy personifications—as Ellmann has shown—
represented oppressed Ireland and oppressive England, respectively. Although the former is endowed with the "sad soul for
ever old and young" of a *fin-de-siècle* hero and although a
general effort is made to intensify the tragic stature of the conflict for its own sake, Yeats is defeated by the patent incredibility of the situation. Gerald Manley Hopkins observed, after
being shown the poem by the proud father, J.B. Yeats:

> Now this *Mosada* I cannot think highly of, but I was happily
> not required then to praise what presumably I had not read,
> and I had read and could praise another piece. It ("The Two
> Titans") was a strained and unworkable allegory about a young

man and a sphinx on a rock in the sea (how did they get there? what did they eat? and so on: people think such criticism very prosaic, but common sense is never out of place anywhere . . .), but still containing fine lines and imagery.[6]

Probably the sort of lines of which Hopkins approved were represented by the closing couplet, with its Shelleyan cosmic violence:

> For ever round thy waking and thy sleep
> The darkness of the whirlwind shattered deep.

Certainly there were promising passages in the poem, but there was also the "abstract" rhetoric which Shelley had used against his political enemies in poems like *Prometheus Unbound* and *Swellfoot the Tyrant*, and which would not have been out of place in the more didactic Young Ireland productions. Such was the judgment on the English sibyl:

> Ignoble joy and more ignoble pain
> Cramm'd all her youth; and hates have bought and sold
> Her spirit. (ll. 12–14)

Over a year later "Ferencz Renyi" appeared in the Boston newspaper *The Pilot*, and in it Yeats manifested a stronger sense of substantiality than before, as cloud parted occasionally to reveal a solid Celtic shore in the distance. The poem is, to be sure, set in Hungary, but Yeats spelled out its relevance to Irish affairs by the addition of a five-line prologue when he included it in *The Wanderings of Oisin and other Poems* in 1889:

> We, too, have seen our bravest and our best
> To prisons go, and mossy ruin rest
> Where homes once whitened vale and mountain crest;
> Therefore, O nation of the bleeding breast,
> Libations from the Hungary of the West.

The plot is concerned with the bravery of a young Hungarian

---

[6] *Further Letters of Gerard Manley Hopkins,* ed. C. C. Abbott (London, 1956).

patriot who watches his loved ones being killed as the price of his refusal to reveal the whereabouts of the rebels, but who at last escapes from his bonds to wreak vengeance upon the Austrian general Haynau who has ordered the execution. Obviously the temptations to melodrama are manifold, and Yeats gives way to them with apparent relish, mitigating whatever gains have been made over "The Two Titans" by an atypical sentimentality reminiscent of Thomas Davis. Indeed, Gurd asserts that the poem is the product of Davis' influence, but if this is so the influence is reflected in the common denominator of raw emotionalism rather than in any aspect of conscious technique. Even in the "Lament for the Death of Eoghan Ruadh O'Neill," which Yeats had somewhat left-handedly praised in his *Tribute to Thomas Davis*, Davis had been unable to conceal his diffuseness with the cloak of Irish history, and there is nothing in his work which suggests the prolonged narrative structure of "Ferencz Renyi." The hand of Young Ireland's guiding spirit could be discerned, or suspected, only in the lingering of Ferencz's eye over homely details like the "brown farmhouse" or the incoherent violence of such outcries as:

> 'Assassin, my assassin! thou who let'st me die,
> I curse thee—curse thee!' (ll. 106–107)

Looking back in his essay "Poetry and Tradition," Yeats admitted that he had never possessed the gift of "speaking political thought in fine verse" (EI, p. 248), but he recognized this gift in a contemporary Anglo-Irishman, Lionel Johnson, who had been a member of the London Irish Literary Society founded by Yeats. Although Johnson's political verses were cast in the same general rhetorical mold as those of the Davis school, they were distinguished by a grandeur reminiscent of the classical ode, a form with which he had become intimately acquainted in his studies at Winchester and Oxford. This classicism enhanced, or was enhanced by, Johnson's deep absorption in the aesthetic dimension of a Catholicism inexorably linked with Ireland. He saw, as Yeats pointed out in the *Autobiographies*, "as one sacred tradition Irish nationality and Catholic religion" (p. 134). Such a judgment is borne out by his major political poem "Ireland," in which the course of Irish history becomes part of the cosmic ritual of God's will and the sorrows of this history are seen, like the death of Christ, as tragic interludes which make possible the triumphant apocalypse. The opening lines show how Johnson's abiding sense of the hieratic elevates his langauge beyond the obvious sentimentality which his subject invites, though it may be that he merely rises into a higher mode of sentimentality:

> Thy sorrow, and the sorrow of the sea,
> Are sisters; the sad winds are of thy race:
> The heart of melancholy beats in thee,
> And the lamenting spirit haunts thy face,
> Mournful and mighty Mother! who are kin
>   To the ancient earth's first woe
> When holy Angels wept, beholding sin.
> For not in penance do thy true tears flow,
> Not thine the long transgression: at thy name,
>   We sorrow not with shame,
> But proudly: for thy soul is as the snow.[7]

In a later stanza Johnson indicates the fallacy of Oisin's legendary contempt for Christian weakness by pointing to the example of the Crusaders: "Signed with the Cross, they conquered and they fell." Here we come to a basic divergence between Johnson and Yeats; the latter felt far greater sympathy for a remote pagan past than he did for a Church which had not been part of his own family heritage. The essay in which he acknowledged Johnson's talent for direct political verse also contains a statement of his own affinity for that divergent stream of Irish literature which treated the traditional matter of myth and legend:

[7] *Poetical Works of Lionel Johnson* (New York, 1915). All subsequent citations of Johnson are to this edition.

I, on the other hand, was more preoccupied with Ireland (for he had other interests), and took from Allingham and Walsh their passion for country spiritism, and from Ferguson his pleasure in heroic legend, and while seeing all in the light of European literature found my symbols of expression in Ireland. (EI, p. 248)

Yeats suggests here not only the division between political poetry and that which reflected ancient Celtic lore but a lesser dichotomy in the latter category which set the mischievous fairies and simple rustics of William Allingham against the massive Gaelic warriors of Sir Samuel Ferguson. The difference in scale was present in style as well as subject, with Allingham choosing to write songs and ballads filled with pleasant local detail while Ferguson was drawn to an epic genre characterized by spacious metaphors and an extended scope of action. Yeats made the two authors perfectly complementary models of technique in his introduction to an anthology which included their works:

> Allingham was the best artist, but Ferguson had the more ample imagination, the more epic aim. . . . He had not the subtlety of feeling, the variety of cadence of a great lyric poet, but he has touched, here and there, an epic vastness and naivety. . . . Allingham is, on the other hand, a master of 'minutely appropriate words', and can wring from the luxurious sadness of the lover, from the austere sadness of old age, the last golden drop of beauty; but amid action and tumult he can but fold his hands.[8]

The contrast is, of course, a little too neat; Allingham's gentleness and limited focus were not quite the same thing as "subtlety of feeling" or the gift for "appropriate words," and Ferguson's ballad "The Fairy Well of Lagnanay" beats Allingham on his own ground. Nonetheless, the respective streams of poetry which these Irishmen represented were distinct enough to split Yeats' own poetic personality during his twenties, thus widening his conception of what constituted "national" poetry.

[8] *A Book of Irish Verse*, ed. W.B. Yeats (London, 1895), pp. xviii–xx.

Gurd claims a little too easily that the two poets exerted no perceptible influence on their young successor's style,[9] and Bloom falls into the same trap with respect to Allingham alone (p. 86). Although Yeats was being typically overgenerous when he wrote to Mrs. Allingham that her husband was his "own master in Irish verse" (L, p. 446), there is little doubt that the approach of the "master" to Irish fairy lore and ballads of the supernatural influenced similar endeavors on Yeats' part and that his reading of Ferguson's *Lays of the Western Gael* "every evening for a short while" (L, p. 61) affected his efforts at that time in the epic genre.

The debt which Yeats acknowledges to Allingham and Walsh for the development of his "passion for country spiritism" has a significance beyond that of a dilettante's interest in provincial ghosts and superstitions. In their treatments of fairy lore he saw, or thought he saw, potentialities for a new imagery which would serve to embody the relation between man and that world of spirit which was always impinging upon his existence. He had suggested this intercourse in *The Island of Statues* with the songs of the disembodied voices, but the Irish spirits, and particularly the fairies, provided ready-made *dramatis personae* at the same time that they linked his work with the spiritualism of the Irish peasantry in which he was trying hard to believe. In the collection of folk tales which he made for the Camelot Series in 1888, he attempted to define the fairies' relation to human life:

> Are they "the gods of the earth?" Perhaps! Many poets, and all mystic and occult writers, in all ages and countries, have declared that behind the visible are chains on chains of conscious beings, who are not of heaven but of the earth, who have no inherent form but change according to their whim, or the mind that sees them. You cannot lift your hand without influencing and being influenced by hoards. The visible world is merely their skin. In dreams we go amongst them, and play with them,

[9] Gurd, p. 15.

and combat them. They are, perhaps, human souls in the crucible—these creatures of whim.[10]

Through the various local exigencies of rhetoric there drifts a constant conception of the fairies as beings occupying a place on the boundary of mortal existence, as between man and whatever limitless powers control his destiny. Their interaction with the lives about whose edges they flit provided minor but easily realized examples of the supernatural drama which was always in progress, whether or not it happened to obtrude itself violently into the narrow range of human perception.

There is small sense of such drama in the poems of Allingham, who makes his fairies trivial by emphasizing their mischievous nature, and delights in pursuing irrelevancies of fairy lore at the expense of his subject. The opening stanza of "The Fairies" exhibits this uninfectious playfulness:

> Up the airy mountain,
>   Down the rushy glen,
> We daren't go a-hunting
>   For fear of little men;
> Wee folk, good folk,
>   Trooping all together;
> Green jacket, red cap,
>   And white owl's feather! [11]

In "Fairy Hill" a particular boy is loved by the fairies. After they feed him with dreams "Of Caves, and Waves, and Moonshine dim" and make him a poet, he falls in love and they celebrate. It is difficult to imagine anything more inconsequential, and it quickly becomes obvious that Allingham is aiming at nothing more ambitious than a pleasant children's song, although the notion of a poet under the guardianship of spirits could have been developed into a study of the nature of inspiration or of the artist's spiritual isolation.

[10] *Fairy and Folk Tales of the Irish Peasantry* (London, 1888), p. 2.
[11] Allingham, *Irish Songs and Poems* (London, 1887). All subsequent citations are to this edition.

Yeats did not altogether escape the baneful influence of such poems. Propelled by a desire to avoid the didacticism of his Irish contemporaries, even as he sought to make his own poetry a part of the very fabric of Ireland, he turned to the "pure" song as one legitimate means of expressing his nationalism. "The Fairy Doctor," which first appeared in 1887 in a letter to Katherine Tynan, is characterized by Allinghamesque simplicity and gentleness, and by the same aimless curiosity about the idiosyncrasies of the Irish spirit world:

> Cures he hath for cow or goat
> With fairy-smitten udders dry—
> Cures for calves with 'plaining throat,
> Staggering with languid eye. (L, p. 50)

It is reassuring to see that Yeats introduced the poem as "these trivial verses," though he reprinted it in *The Wanderings of Oisin and other Poems* and discoursed learnedly on "fairy doctors" in *Fairy and Folk Tales of the Irish Peasantry*.

In another light, the mere choice of fairy personae was part of a larger attempt on the part of Yeats to forge an aesthetic link with that Irish peasantry for whose sensitivity and perceptiveness he retained such a high regard, and the fact that many of the episodes involving these personae are cast as ballads shows that the attempt extended to considerations of form as well as content. The late spring and summer of 1887 brought with it a rash of ballad-writing on the part of the Young Irelanders as they began to collect material for their volume. A group of letters to Katherine Tynan during this period indicates the extent of Yeats' own activities in this genre. He continually sent his efforts to her and O'Leary for approval; it is amusing to find the latter dissenting in the case of a ballad about a Sligo madwoman which he considered "morbid" (L, p. 37).

Such dissent was rare, however, among the ephoebes and their sage; generally, if a ballad were based upon a story from the folk-imagination and told in simple language which reflected its origins, then it could be supposed to take its place among the true productions of the heart. The old Wordsworth- ian theory of diction from the 1800 preface to *Lyrical Ballads*, with its emphasis on "the real language of men," seems to rear its head when Yeats writes of his lyric "The Lamentation of the Old Pensioner": "This small poem is little more than a transla- tion into verse of the very words of an old Wicklow peasant" (VE, p. 799). Indeed, the plot of a poem like "The Ballad of Moll Magee" might well have been by Wordsworth, who also treated the matter of maternal suffering in "The Thorn" and "The Mad Mother." Both poets use "simple" diction and con- centrate upon evoking the pathos of a peasant mother's mis- fortune rather than attempting to give the misfortune tragic form and treat it in perspective, and both fall noticeably below the standards which they set when they allowed their linguis- tic sophistication free rein upon more congenial subject matter.

Richard Ellmann points out, rightly, that Yeats failed in the early ballad experiments; but the exact nature of his strictures in a contrast of "The Ballad of Moll Magee" with "Father Gilligan" must be examined:

> In the first . . . Yeats is aiming at a folk ballad, though the sim- plicity does not ring true, especially in an inversion like 'fisher poor'. In the second he attempts an artificial, literary ballad with equal maladroitness. . . . Each style seems slightly contaminated by the other, as if he did not yet fully understand either. (*Masks*, pp. 142–143)

There is no denying the illegitimacy of "Moll Magee" as a folk ballad; not only does it contain artificial inversions, but it uti- lizes a dramatic monologue form. Nor is Ellmann wrong in asserting that Yeats alternated during this period between a literary style and a more popular one. What is doubtful is that "Father Gilligan" is "literary" in the sense that this term would apply to poems like "King Goll" or "The Wanderings of Oisin." It is, on the contrary, part of the same effort as "Moll Magee" to circumvent the exclusiveness of the "coteries" by telling peasant legends in a language and progression which suggested neither complexity nor artificiality, even if Yeats does not always avoid such suggestion.

The dialect which Yeats utilizes in "Moll Magee," and which no doubt encouraged Ellmann's contrast, was a nonce experiment; its occasional occurrence afterward in a poem such as "Father O'Hart," [12] which is placed immediately after "Father Gilligan" in *The Countess Kathleen and other Poems*, shows that it was merely an unfortunate device for enhancing the Irish flavoring of ballads which shared a basic community of style. Just how "literary" in a pejorative sense the story of Father Gilligan could be may be seen from its treatment at the hands of a forgotten poet named Tristram St. Martin, whose poem "He sent His Angel" was published shortly before Yeats' own. The first stanza, for example, runs:

> One dull grey evening in the autumn time
> A parish priest approached his cottage door
> Fordone with toil; for it was his to climb
> Each day the steep hill-path and cross the rugged moor.[13]

Yeats's opening, on the other hand, is less stilted and artificial, and shows a keener sense of the rhythm, syntax, and diction appropriate to the narrative of folk tale:

> The old priest Peter Gilligan
> Was weary night and day
> For half his flocks were in their beds
> Or under green sods lay.

In the work of Allingham Yeats had found examples of both

[12] Yeats gaelicizes his original by the insertion of words like "shoneen" and "Sleiveens." This original was T. O'Rorke's *History, Antiquities, and Present State of the Parishes of Ballysodare and Kilvarnet* (Dublin, 1878).

[13] Tristram St. Martin, *The Christ in London and other Poems* (London, 1890). See *Letters*, p. 206, for Yeats' rather huffy reply to "Anonymous correspondent," who had apparently implied in *The Academy* that "Father Gilligan" was plagiarized from St. Martin's poem.

Wordsworthian faith in natural man and ballads on the Irish clergy. The earlier poet had constantly celebrated, as Yeats pointed out, the small, insignificant beauties of his own provincial surroundings. In one of his more ambitious poems, "The Music Master," he emphasized the ethical benefits of these surroundings and the tragedy of their being left behind by a young man who wandered out into the alien world and returned to find his childhood sweetheart dead. Here, however, the style is more like that of "Michael" than that of "The Thorn," for it is shot through with the sententious involutions of eighteenth-century moral rhetoric.

More important, perhaps, was the prototype which Allingham's "The Abbot of Inisfalen" provided for "The Priest and the Fairy," "Father Gilligan," and "Father O'Hart." Subtitled *A Killarney Legend*, it describes how the Abbot wakes from a sleep into which he had fallen in the woodland and returns to the abbey to encounter only strangers from whom he hears "The foreign tongue of the Sassenach, not wholesome Irish speech." Upon learning that he has slept for two hundred years and has wakened to an Ireland which has fallen upon "an evil day," he asks for absolution and dies peacefully as two white birds sing a glorious song outside the casement.

The emphasis upon the strangeness of miracle, the portrayal of the cleric as a man of great blessedness and sanctity, the use of nature's gentler aspects as signs of God's grace, and incremental repetition such as the five "Low kneeled . . . " clauses are all found in Yeats's clerical ballads, which deal with various legendary anecdotes. A priest encounters a fairy in the isolated countryside and is asked about the fate of fairies' souls; the weary Father Gilligan falls asleep after he has been summoned to give extreme unction and, upon waking, rides frantically to the dead man's house to find that an angel of the Lord has appeared in his stead to render the service; while Father O'Hart, in the most inconsequential tale of all, stamps out the heathen custom of keening and is himself keened upon his death by the birds of the air as a last reproof to those who had been guilty of such incongruous mourning.

Yeats asserted in "The Stirring of the Bones" that he had "simplified" his style after "The Wanderings of Oisin" by filling his "imagination with country stories" (A, p. 223). There is no question but that he was never again quite so ornate and exotic as in *The Island of Statues* and certain passages of "Oisin," and his proficiency in the art of narrative developed quickly after the sporadic flow of "Ferencz Renyi." Ballad-writing, however, although it certainly played its part in these improvements, was essentially a mistaken path so far as it attempted to meet the "people" upon their own linguistic and conceptual grounds. The uncharacteristic triteness of phrase and the poverty of thought of the ballads demonstrate just how disastrous it would have been had Yeats neglected the polish and complexity of the art represented by "The Wanderings of Oisin" for some Wordsworthian sense of mission.

Fortunately the popular lore also contained legends and mythical personae more susceptible to the serious and sophisticated treatment of the supernatural which had characterized Yeats' literary efforts almost from the first. We have seen in an examination of "The Seeker" and the last act of *The Island of Statues* how he could at least suggest the aesthetic potentialities of a focus upon the drama of man's involvement with the inhuman forces which encompass him, and in the Irish preoccupation with these forces he found scope for the development of this drama. Since the fairies were regarded as creatures of the boundary between mortal existence and the existence beyond, they provided—as suggested above—a possible source of *dramatis personae*. There was, of course, no escaping the connotations of frivolity which inevitably attached to them and which Allingham had exploited in various playful verses. Yeats himself had indulged such a penchant in poems like "The Fairy Doctor" and "The Priest and the Fairy," and it is not surprising that he soon rejected the fairies in favor of a more formidable cast.

Nonetheless they figure in several poems as forces to be reckoned with, and their capriciousness and joy are occasionally placed in an emotional perspective which lends them a significance largely absent from Allingham's work. Even in a bagatelle like "The Fairy Pedant" Yeats manages to build up a conflict between a typical airy existence and the incursion of a heavy introspection which deepens the character even as it dries up the conventional wellsprings of happiness. Although it is obscured by the preciosity of the imagery, there is a resemblance between the emotion of the isolated Second Fairy and Romantic *angst*.

The most important theme which Yeats got from Irish fairy lore was that of the abduction of a mortal by a supernatural being. In this theme, a natural outgrowth of the daemonic, were the seeds for a vivid study of the ambiguities surrounding man's attempt to escape from the fortuity of earthly emotion to some Nirvana in which the circumstances of happiness remain constant. "An Indian Song" had been no more than a simple affirmation of the possibility of such an escape, but as early as "The Stolen Child," which appeared in the Young Ireland volume of 1888, Yeats was adopting a more complex view. The Irish tradition was itself unresolved upon the point of whether the abducted persons indeed enjoyed contentment; Allingham had suggested that they did not in a casual account of an abduction in "The Fairies," which was really more preoccupied with the vagaries of fairy behavior than with spiritual realities. Ferguson does not mention the transfigured state of Una, heroine of "The Fairy Well of Lagnanay," who voluntarily enters Faery after disappointment in a love affair. The treatment, as one might expect from Ferguson, sticks very close to tradition, with emphasis on the ceremony which Una performs and upon the use of the magic plants such as hawthorn and bracken by which the characters of medieval romance had entered the Otherworld.

It is, in fact, characteristic of Yeats that he should dramatize the emotional conflict which movement between the two worlds involves by writing a fairy song which describes the changed life and reactions of the mortal, and which adds to the sheer terror or delight of the situation a moral dimension. Edward Walsh had written a song called "The Fairy Nurse" but it had contained no effort to emphasize the spiritual gap with which the sleeping child would have to cope upon awaking, and the persona herself, with her maternal instincts, could just as well be a quite human nanny as a supernatural being. In "The Stolen Child," however, a paradise rather similar to the earlier Arcady is represented as a place of mindless joy far preferable to a world which is, as each refrain reiterates, "more full of weeping than you can understand." Activities such as whispering evil dreams into the ear of a trout are uncomfortably reminiscent of Allingham, but Yeats manages to invest the totality of these activities with something of the spirit of Oberon's kingdom, a translucent world "Where the wave of moonlight glosses / The dim grey sands with light." Such an existence offers a vivid contrast to that more substantial life which the child is leaving:

> He'll hear no more the lowing
> Of the calves on the warm hillside,
> Or the kettle on the hob
> Sing peace into his breast,
> Or see the brown mice bob
> Round and round the oatmeal chest.

It is really this stanza which gives the poem its touch of richness and rescues it from the category of "Flight . . . from the real world" (L, p. 63) to which Yeats consigned it in a moment of despair. This particular selection of details from the child's accustomed life, as critics have noted, leaves no doubt that an enveloping warmth and familiarity must be left behind if he is to participate in the more ethereal joys praised in the preceding stanzas. There is something ominous in the fairies' invitation which was not present in that of the Indian, and we must recall the disadvantages of a seemingly utopian state which are made explicit by Naschina's transfiguration and by the damning answer given to the question about eternal life in "The Priest and the Fairy."

Yeats' most extended and complex treatment of a mortal's voyage to Faery is, of course, "The Wanderings of Oisin," which he completed in 1888. The poem is, in fact, a repository or paradigm of almost every motif which had previously interested him; and this diversity is hardly surprising in light of the fact that he had been engaged upon it, if his memory is accurate,[14] since 1886. According to Russell Alspach,[15] who has compared Yeats' vague references to his sources with extant manuscripts, the main original is "The Lay of Oisin on the Land of Youth," by the eighteenth-century Gaelic poet Michael Comyn. Of the two translations available, a comparison with Yeats' version shows that he almost certainly used the one done by Bryan O'Looney for the Ossianic Society.[16] The same volume of the Society's *Transactions*, along with volumes I and III, provided him with a translation of "The middle Irish dialogues of St. Patrick and Usheen" which he mentions as an additional source in a note to the 1895 edition of his poetry.

Alspach points up various similarities and differences in detail between Yeats and Comyn, but does not seek in Yeats' changes any consistent principle of selection which would explain what larger design the later poet had in mind, beyond quoting Yeats' own statement to the effect that he was seeking

[14] See footnote no. 13, chap. I.
[15] R.K. Alspach, "Some Sources of Yeats's *The Wanderings of Oisin*," *PMLA*, LVIII (1943), 849–866.
[16] *Transactions of the Ossianic Society, for the Year 1856*, IV (Dublin, 1859), 230–279.

to create a "natural literature." What in fact does emerge from a comparison of the two versions is that Yeats consistently shaped his material to emphasize the interaction of Oisin's humanity with various manifestations of a superhuman paradise; whereas Comyn, passing casually over the dramatic moments in which two modes of being clashed, demonstrated that determination to get on with the adventure or the sensuous catalogue which had earlier characterized the medieval romance. The tradition and the paradise themselves had certain archetypal features which antedated both Yeats and Comyn by a number of centuries; this fact may be seen in Alfred Nutt's description of the "salient features of the Happy Otherworld as portrayed in Bran's Voyage":

> It may be reached by mortals specially summoned by denizens of the land; the summons comes from a damsel, whose approach is marked by magically sweet music, and who bears a magic apple-branch. She describes the land under the most alluring colours—its inhabitants are free from death and decay, they enjoy in full measure a simple round of sensuous delights, the land itself is one of thrice fifty distant isles lying to the west of Ireland; access to the whole group is guarded by Manannan, son of Lir.[17]

This, the general introduction to the *Tir na nOg* myth, is common to both poets, but Yeats makes a radical change in Comyn's version when he has Oisin and Niamh go directly to the Island of the Living rather than stop to effect the conventional rescue of a distressed maiden. The alteration makes for a much more emphatic transition on Oisin's part from the sad, listless hunt in the aftermath of a slaughter of Fenian companions to the island paradise where he and Niamh were greeted by:

> . . . a band
> Of youths and maidens hand in hand
> And singing, singing all together. (I, 201–203)

[17] Kuno Meyer and Alfred Nutt, *The Voyage of Bran* (London, 1895–97) I, pp. 142–143.

Yeats also drops the ceremonial meeting which Comyn's Oisin has with the king and queen of the island; his own island has no rulers, and its life is centered upon idyllic pastoral pursuits rather than the organized splendors of courtly life which had appealed so powerfully to medieval audiences. "Joy" is celebrated as the ultimate value in the song of the "young man":

> For joy the little planets run
> Round us, and rolls the unwieldy sun.
> If joy were nowhere on the earth
> There were an end of change and birth;
> The universe herself would die,
> And in some urn funereal lie
> Folded like a frozen fly. (I, 267–273)

The nature of this joy is perhaps more complex than it at first appears, for when Oisin lifts a harp to sing of "human joy" the immortals weep and throw "the saddest harp in all the world" into a pool. Yeats suggests here that human joy, because it derives its warmth from the flesh, must inevitably capitulate before death and is thus incompatible with the joy of eternity. A variant of the principle quoted above from the essay on Spenser, with its opposition of "passion" to "dateless leisure and unrepining peace," seems to be operating, but Yeats enriches his thesis in this instance by dramatizing the onslaught of Oisin's discontent with this pleasant but enervated existence. Coming upon the shaft of some "dead warrior's lance" washed up by the tide, the Fenian is overwhelmed by the remembered exhilaration of comradeship in battle, and Niamh realizes that the "human sadness" has returned.

Comyn's poem had also dealt with Oisin's nostalgia for his comrades as a target for St. Patrick's taunts, and with his return to a Christianized Ireland where he was bereft not only of his long-dead kinsmen but of the hope for immortality. Here the important difference lies in Yeats' treatment of this nostalgia as an important thematic element, and in his extension of the voyage to two more islands of yet further significance in man's quest for an ideal existence. The whole has a moral dimension lacking in Comyn's simple tale of love and adventure, which does not get far beyond the naive delights of "Sir Orfeo" or "King Horn."

Yeats himself indicated the complexity of his intentions in a letter to Katherine Tynan:

> 'Oisin' needs an interpreter. There are three incompatible things which man is always seeking—infinite feeling, infinite battle, infinite repose—hence the three islands. (L, p. 111)

The operative word here is "infinite"; all three states may be enjoyed in temporary measure in the worldly life of the warrior, but he inevitably wishes to enjoy all of them shorn of the limitations of the finite. Since the infinity of one state must rule out that of another, the wish is self-contradictory, and the vision of the transient but multifarious conditions of an earlier existence rises constantly up to tempt Oisin with a warmth and richness which he has foregone as the price of a narrow eternity.

The poem is patterned to lead inescapably back to this theme of an entirely human life which is shot through with insecurity and vague discontents, but is nonetheless more complete than any paradise experienced under the auspices of the pagan supernatural or promised by the representatives of Christianity. The proviso must be added, however, that the particular life of the Fenians for which Oisin longs has its own element of the paradisiacal. The spear shaft urges the hero on to a hundred years of battle, ended by the appearance of a beech bough which recalls the joys of repose:

> Remembering how I paced in days gone o'er
> At Eman, 'neath the beech trees, on each side,
> Fin, Conan, Oscar, many more, the tide
> Of planets watching, watching the race of hares
> Leap in the meadow. (II, 227–229)

Similarly, at the conclusion of the next hundred years of sleep and languorous semi-consciousness Oisin sees:

> A starling—like them that foregathered 'neath
> A moon waking white as a shell,
> When the Fenians may foray at morning
> With Bran, Sgeolan, Lomair. (III, 103–104)

The possibilities of "infinite" states of pleasure outside mortal life having been exhausted, it is here that the voyage begins to come full circle as Oisin longs to return to the wakefulness of the "foray" from which he was first called by Niamh. This return is, however, impossible since the element of infinity cannot coexist with mortal joys, and Oisin himself falls prey to the penalty of those who choose the temporal world.

Bloom has some excellent insights into the poem's larger theme, which he convincingly relates to the Romantic tradition of the antithetical quester; but he brings up some arguable points and implications when he asserts that:

> Yeats ends the poem, not with Shelley's impressively cold farewell to nature, as in *Alastor*, but by going past nature to a choice between finalities: swordsman and saint, Oisin and Patrick, the stones of the fire and the glance of the saved. Oisin, after death, will "dwell in the house of the Fenians, be they in flames or at feast." (p. 102)

It is not at all clear that to choose the role of "swordsman" is to go "past nature." Oisin's eternity will be spent with the Fenians, who are identified with nature (as opposed to supernature) throughout the poem. By choosing their company he is affirming his solidarity with aspiring man, who is trapped in nature's mortality yet perfers the rich humanity of this tragic lot to the "salvation" of the sterile utopias beyond nature. If Shelley's farewell to nature is "impressively cold," then Yeats' affirmation here is impressively warm in its anticipation of the prevailing argument in "A Dialogue of Self and Soul." Death and even the flames of hell, like the "fecund ditch" and the agonies of life's stages in the later poem, are worth enduring in light of the reward which the purely human is in itself. It is true that Oisin's fall from his horse into mortality is an accident, but the deep nostalgia which pulled him back toward nature was not; and the conscious rejection of Patrick's heaven enhances the element of choice behind the rejection of Niamh's pagan paradises.

The fact that Yeats has a larger purpose in "Oisin," that the myth is taken beyond its function as adventure story and used as the vehicle for a fairly complex ethical study, reveals immediately a crucial difference between the poet and his Irish contemporaries in the treatment of material from their common tradition. This larger purpose, however, seems to have escaped Dorothy Hoare in her book *The Works of Morris and Yeats in Relation to Early Saga Literature*. She dismisses it as a "curious production . . . written almost entirely for the sake of embroidery," [18] and insists that it is strongly influenced by Morris' *Earthly Paradise*, although Yeats confessed in the *Autobiographies* that he had not read Morris for some years when that venerable poet complimented him upon writing "my kind of poetry." Since the standards she applies are those of primitive Irish saga, it is hardly curious that she finds in it, along with other of Yeats's early works, "a movement away from life to fantasy." Miss Hoare did not have the advantage of knowing that Yeats had used a translation of an eighteenth-century Gaelic poem as a source, and she gives his own invention perhaps more blame for the "dream" elements than it deserves, although there is no doubt but that the Celtic twilight makes Yeats' version far less athletic than any early epic.

Even if her premises are admitted, however, Yeats finds some warrant for his treatment of Irish legend in no less an authority than W. P. Ker, who views the ancient verses as being somewhat less realistic and prosaic than does Miss Hoare:

> If . . . the imagination of the Northern mythologists was dominated by the thought of the fall of the gods, the day when Odin meets with the wolf, the Celts have given their hearts to the enchanted ground, to the faery magic, in many stories of adven-

[18] Dorothy Hoare, *The Works of Morris and Yeats in Relation to Early Saga Literature* (Cambridge, 1937), pp. 113–114.

tures in the underworld and voyages westward to an island paradise.[19]

Yeats himself quoted Ker in his review of Lady Gregory's *Cuchulain of Muirthemne*, praising his distinction between the Norse and Irish tempers as "epical and romantic" [20] respectively rather than "dramatic and lyrical" as Morris had said.

Lady Gregory's book, which Yeats insisted was "the best book to come out of Ireland in my time," had not been published until 1901, and for his direct knowledge of Irish epic the poet was still dependent upon miscellaneous translations and treatises such as Standish O'Grady's *History of Ireland*. However, extended treatments of the epic material were available in the poetry of Sir Samuel Ferguson, a poet who was greatly respected in Ireland during the late nineteenth century, and who—as an antidote to Allingham—did much to form the conception of the heroic so crucial to the make-up of the later Yeatsian personae. He is generally dismissed by modern commentators as prosaic and unimaginative,[21] but some of the same qualities which led to this judgment became, through an earlier generation's eyes, evidence of a praiseworthy "distinct symmetrical outline" and a lack of "morbid poetic appetite." [22] Although aware of the absence of exquisite detail and romantic delicacy in his work, Yeats had admired his massive lines and grasp of heroic scope; he was particularly impressed by the "epic vastness" * of one of Ferguson's similes in "Congal," where the cloak of a striding giant is described:

> A mantle, skirted stiff with soil splashed from
> the miry ground,

[19] Quoted by B.J.C. Grierson in *Lyrical Poetry from Blake to Hardy* (London, 1928), p. 150.

[20] *Explorations* (London, 1962), p. 8.

[21] See Hoare, p. 112; and A. Norman Jeffares, *W. B. Yeats: Man and Poet* (London, 1949), p. 45.

[22] Aubrey De Vere, quoted by A.P. Graves in *A Treasury of Irish Poetry*, ed. S.A. and T.W. Rolleston (London, 1900), p. 277.

* See above, p. 57.

> At every stride against his calves struck with as
>   loud rebound
> As makes the mainsail of a ship brought up along
>   the blast,
> When with the coil of all its ropes it beats the
>   sounding mast.[23]

It is quite possible that this "vastness" influenced Yeats' conception of the giant figures on the Isle of Victories, though these had—as we have seen—antecedents in Shelley, who preceeded Ferguson by several years in Yeats' reading. A probable echo of Ferguson has been found by both Jeffares and Alspach[24] in Oisin's reference to "Oscar's pencilled urn" (I, 22). The relevant passage from "Aidenn's Grave" runs:

> The great green rath's ten-acred tomb
> Lies heavy on his urn.
> A cup of bodkin-pencilled clay
> Holds Oscar. . . .

Despite this lone specific similarity, the "embroideries" of "The Wanderings of Oisin" make it clear that Ferguson's preoccupation with overall design had not yet been fully assimilated. It is more likely that he exerted some influence on Yeats' narrative meters, no less than three of which appear in "Oisin" in interesting correspondence with the varying nature of the subject matter. The visit to the Isle of the Living, with its romantic abduction and exotic pursuits, is narrated in swiftly moving tetrameters which are not unlike those of Ferguson in "Aidenn's Grave," although each quatrain of the latter closes with a trimeter. Compare, for instance, Yeats:

> 'Tis sad remembering, sick with years,
> The swift, innumerable spears,

---

[23] *Poems of Sir Samuel Ferguson*, intro. A. P. Graves (Dublin, 1916). All subsequent citations of Ferguson are to this edition.
[24] See Jeffares, p. 45; and Alspach, *PMLA*, pp. 859–860.

> The long-haired warriors, the spread feast;
> And love, in the hours when youth had ceased . . .
>
> (I, 5–7a)

with Ferguson:

> They heaved the stone; they heap'd the cairn:
> Said Ossian, 'In a queenly grave
> We leave her, 'mong her fields of fern,
> Between the cliff and wave'.

Yeats is, of course, intentionally more irregular, but this use of the four-beat line for the extended narration of myth is unprecedented in his work, and argues a possible model such as Ferguson's poem could have provided.

The meter of the second book of "Oisin" changes to heroic couplets in keeping with the new theme of "infinite battle," while in the third book the Island of Forgetfulness is described in the most languorous hexameters imaginable. Despite this obvious attempt at differentiating the last two episodes there is a certain community of rhythmical style between them, and it seems to derive in part from the large number of trochaic and dactylic substitutions and involuted phrasings. The appearance in Book III, for instance, of the verb-subject inversion already noted in the "Island of Victories" episode awakens echoes of the "Ferencz Renyi" style which are intensified by other distortions of normal phrasings:

> But in dreams, mild man of the crosiers, driving
>   the dust with their throngs,
> Moved round me, of seamen or landsmen, all who
>   are winter tales;
> Came by me the kings of the Red Branch with roaring
>   of laughter and songs,
> Or moved as they moved once, love-making
>   or piercing the tempest with sails.
>
> (III, 85–88)

Compare the following lines from Ferguson's "Conary":

> Banished the land of Erin, on the sea
> They roamed, and roaming, with the pirate-hordes
> Of British Ingcel leagued; and this their pact:
> The spoil of Britain's and of Alba's coasts
> To fall to them; and Erin's counter-spoil
> To fall to Ingcel. Britain's borders first
> They ravaged; and in one pernicious raid
> Of sack and slaughter indiscriminate,
> Ingcel's own father and his brethren seven
> By chance sojourning with the victims, slew.

Ferguson is obviously echoing the grand epic style represented by Milton's Latinate phrasings, and it would seem that the young Yeats is in turn torturing his own syntax into a lesser degree of that involution which the master of Irish epic apparently considered a part of "vast design." It was no doubt the style of the last two books of "Oisin" which led a *Manchester Guardian* reviewer to call Yeats "a rough and sometimes harmonious bard" but to praise him at the same time for lacking the "facile gift of music" which had ruined Thomas Moore and other Irish poets.[25]

Ferguson's true forte lay in the description of heroic ventures rather than the more exotic and romantic tangents of Irish mythology, since his spare, matter-of-fact style lent a certain dignified coldness to such efforts. This order had been reversed by Yeats in "The Wanderings of Oisin," where the heroic motif—although predominant in Book II—was only one of several which ran through a basically romantic reach for the eternal conditions of paradise. Only three years later, however, the appearance of "The Death of Cuchullin" * showed Yeats making an attempt to purify his "epic" style of those elements of fantasy which interfered with the cold and detached vision of

[25] "*The Wanderings of Oisin and other Poems*," anon. rev., *The Manchester Guardian*, Jan 28, 1889.
* Later re-titled "Cuchulain's Fight with the Sea."

the hero's action, and it is here that the example of Ferguson comes into its own. Portions of "Oisin" had been repositories of the "reds and yellows" which offended Yeats, and in "Cuchullin" he concentrated fiercely upon the outline of the tragic pattern, falling only occasionally back into the old softness as he spoke of Cuchulain's son "Driving the deer along the woody ways," or of Cuchulain's eyes "more mournful than the depth of starry skies."

It is strange that "The Death of Cuchullin" should suffer at the hands of Miss Hoare the same perfunctory dismissal as an "empty" poetry of "reverie" (p. 116) which she had accorded to "The Wanderings of Oisin." The characters have only the slightest traces of the static about them, and show no sign of a desire to exchange their earthly situations for any sort of dream-world. Even that degree of removal from "reality" which Oisin's recounting of his adventures had effected vanished in the dialogue and third-person narrative of the later poem. One can only assume that the definition of "freshly felt and communicated emotion" which Miss Hoare has derived from the primitive Irish saga does not admit of such artificial elements as a conscious shaping of the story for an effect of heightened tragedy.

That Yeats has indulged in such a shaping is obvious from a comparison of his poem with its prose source "Cuculin" in Jeremiah Curtin's *Myths and Folklore of Ireland*.[26] Curtin merely alludes to Emer's jealousy, but Yeats dramatizes her realization that Cuchulain has deserted her for another by the episode of Aileel the swineherd, who is unmentioned in the original. Emer's outcry upon learning of Cuchulain's return; the trembling of Aileel as he hesitantly tells of the new mistress; and finally Emer's order to beat him with "thongs of leather"— all these indicate effectively the first rumblings of the tragic crescendo and lend credibility to Emer's role as the catalyst of doom. Again, the earlier version has Emer informing her son of

[26] The revelant pages are 324–326. See VE, p. 799, for Yeats' citation.

Cuchulain's identity, with the result that he consciously avoids killing him and is himself killed by the father, who has not yet recognized him. Yeats was obviously aware of the mitigation of the tragedy which this knowledge effected, and makes each protagonist unaware of the other's identity so that final focus is solely upon the awakening of Cuchullin's recognition and its aftermath.

In a sense "Cuchulain's Fight with the Sea" represented the climax of Yeats' period of "simplification" after 1886. He had passed through the pitfalls of Irish propaganda and Irish trivia to reach at least the outskirts of the tragic plateau in a stark unsentimental presentation of heroic legend. This virile simplicity, however, was achieved at the expense of a lessening of the thematic spaciousness which had earlier marked "The Wanderings of Oisin." In its very escape from allegorical complexity the later poem had swung back toward the level of the well-told adventure, and away from universality. Perhaps sensing this, Yeats was already beginning, in 1892, the return to what might be called "cosmic scope" in his poems on the mystic Rose and other arcane phenomena—subject matter adumbrated by his interest in the precise apparatus of "Tall wands of alder and white quicken wands" which the Druids used to enchant Cuchulain. Nonetheless, he would carry into his new period of complexity a clearer conception of heroic character and a sense of the potentialities of Irish myth which would bear fruit for the rest of his career, and which are directly traceable to his early attempt to come to terms with his Celtic legacy.

III

The Late Victorian Context

THE NATIONALISTIC FERVOR OF THE LATE EIGHT-
ies had temporarily obscured for Yeats his close links with the
English literary tradition which furnished his first formative
influences. These influences, to be sure, had come in large part
from past stages of that tradition, but with the founding of the
Rhymers' Club in 1891 Yeats was brought into close contact
with its late Victorian stage as embodied in such contemporaries as Ernest Dowson, Arthur Symons, and Lionel Johnson,
the last of whom Yeats had already known for several years.
Longer and longer periods of residence in London and increasing publication of his reviews and poems brought Yeats to the
attention of literati who were bound to compare him with
Tennyson and Browning on the one hand, and with the Pre-
Raphaelites and their *fin-de-siècle* successors on the other. The
comparison is necessary for us, as well, if we are to define Yeats'
position in the late nineteenth century and separate those portions of the matrix which helped to form his entire artistic
generation from those such as the occult societies which encouraged his uniqueness.

In the case of the "great Victorians," of course, this comparison turns out to be essentially a contrast. The Rhymers,

who could disagree over various poetical techniques, were united in their opposition to the aesthetic climate which succeeded Tennyson's earlier poetry, and Yeats gets down to specifics in the famous passage from his introduction to *The Oxford Book of Modern Verse*:

> The revolt against Victorianism meant to the young poet a revolt against irrelevant descriptions of nature, the scientific and moral discursiveness of *In Memoriam*—'When he should have been broken-hearted,' said Verlaine, 'he had many reminiscences'—the political eloquence of Swinburne, the psychological curiosity of Browning, and the poetical diction of everybody.[1]

This revolt was made articulate in the conversations and meetings of the Rhymers' Club; but it had been in progress, if we may judge by Yeats' actions, for several years. In 1885 for instance, while Tennyson desperately sought grounds for optimism in a world "dark with griefs and graves" and Browning continued to search the labyrinth of character for traces of immortality, Yeats was finishing up the series of exotic poems about sorceresses, shepherds, and enchanted islands, and embarking upon an apparently serious study of Irish fairy lore.

The way had been cleared over thirty years before by the Pre-Raphaelites, who eschewed involvement with contemporary social issues and psychological realism in favor of subject matter deliberately chosen for remoteness in time and atmosphere from a prosaic present. They had built up in their modified Romantic vein a body of poetry substantial enough to offer the stimulus and encouragement of a positive tradition to the young poets of the Nineties who wished to re-emphasize the ascendancy of the purely aesthetic in literature. More than one of this generation must have styled themselves, as did the twenty-year-old Yeats, "in all things pre-Raphaelite" (A, p. 70).

In Yeats' case, however, this catchall description obscures

[1] (Oxford, 1936), p. ix.

perhaps as much as it reveals. For one thing, his own variety of Victorian Romanticism was in part the outgrowth of individual access to the early nineteenth-century fountainhead; while there is no denying his general acquiescence in the *fin-de-siècle* vitiation exhibited by the later works of Morris, it is evident that he frequently displays that powerful sense of the autonomous existence of a supernatural order which suggests the daemonic realms of Shelley and Coleridge rather than the idealized medieval order dear to the Pre-Raphaelites.

Bloom hits near the heart of the matter when he points out that:

> In *Crossways*, the poet moves . . . with the fierce urgency of the High Romantics modulated into the overtly baffled longing of their Pre-Raphaelite disciples, Rossetti and Morris. . . . Yeats inherits from Rossetti and Morris their doomed attempt to render phantasmagoria as though it were nature, finding realistic detail in imaginary contexts. (p. 106)

The point is that this nature painting is identified, as has been shown, with Yeats' earliest phase and that the Romantic "urgency," entering with the "cloud and foam" of the Tynan letter, reduces Pre-Raphaelite solidity and stasis to a minimum by the early Nineties. Yeats' real debts to the Pre-Raphaelites were specifically for the image of a peculiar type of womanhood and the concept of a cult devoted to this type; generally for their development of a second Victorian tradition which stressed the aesthetic over the purely moralistic.

The radicalism of Yeats' "Romantic" position is explained not only by his natural bias and his youthful absorption in Shelley, but by certain factors which push Rossetti and Morris closer than he to the shadow of Tennyson. To begin with, Tennyson himself had provided an important prototype for the romantic medievalism of the Pre-Raphaelites in his early poetry. J. W. Mackail relates how this poetry swept all before it in the Oxford of the 1850's, when that city was the seed-bed of Pre-Raphaelitism. The young Morris, an undergraduate at

Exeter, proclaimed Tennyson's ballad "Oriana" the "finest and most epical" of his work, but there was general agreement that a decline had set in after Maud, "his last poem that really mattered." [2] Dismissing Tennyson's Sir Galahad as "rather a mild youth," Morris established the limits of the older poet's usefulness, and implied that he who seeks the *Zeitgeist* of the Middle Ages cannot sacrifice the notes of wildness and vigor to the sort of Victorian gentility which led Swinburne to refer snidely to "Tennyson's *Morte D'Albert.*"

It was precisely these notes which Morris had heard in "Oriana," and which had led him to term that poem "epical." The "damned arrow" which pierces the heart of Oriana; the "deathbed stabs" of the battle; the piping of the "Norland wind"—all these suggested a bleak, violent world related to that of the Norse and Anglo-Saxon heroic poetry which Morris would later attempt to revive. More immediately, the brutal directness of Tennyson's lines:

> They should have stabbed me where I lay,
> Oriana—
> They should have trod me into clay,
> Oriana. . . . [3]

was surely carried over into Morris' "The Haystack in the Floods":

> . . . so then
> Godmar turn'd grinning to his men,
> Who ran, some five or six, and beat
> His head to pieces at their feet.[4]

Another aspect of Tennyson's medievalism which attracted

[2] J.W. Mackail, *The Life of William Morris* (London, New York and Bombay, 1899), pp. 44–46.

[3] Alfred Tennyson, *Poetical Works* (London, 1954). All subsequent citations of Tennyson are to this edition.

[4] *The Collected Works of William Morris* (London, New York, and Bombay, 1910) I. All subsequent citations of Morris are to this edition and this volume.

Morris and Rossetti as well, was the picturesque, decorative mode of such poems as "Mariana" and "The Lady of Shalott." Here we have the stylized, tapestry-like world of Arthurian chivalry, a world into which Mariana is made to fit despite her Renaissance credentials. The "flower pots," "rusted nails," and "silver-green" poplar of her "lonely moated grange" possess an air of homeliness rendered poignant and romantic by the distancing of antiquity, and it is precisely this air for which Morris is striving in his depiction of the castle of "Golden Wings":

> Many scarlet bricks there were
> In its walls, and old grey stone;
> Over which red apples shone
> At the right time of the year.

Rossetti inclined more towards the formalized, quasi-religious vein of courtly love and there is no question that he found in "The Lady of Shalott" a Tennysonian prototype for the heroine of "The Staff and Scrip":

> The Queen sat idle by her loom:
>   She heard the arras stir,
> And looked up sadly: through the room
>   The sweetness sickened her
>   Of musk and myrrh.[5]

What is important is that both epic temper and predilection for the antique picturesque may be seen as part of an established English tendency towards emphasis upon the specifically human—as opposed to superhuman—aspects of the Middle Ages. As early as Malory, one may see the "humanizing" of the Arthurian legends into a narrative more concerned with the practicalities of combining the violent martial talents with such social virtues of loyalty, courtesy, and pity, than with the aesthetic exploitation of magical and spiritual phenomena. The de-

[5] *The Poems of Dante Gabriel Rossetti* (New York, 1923) I. All subsequent citations of Rossetti are to this edition.

light in the arcane which had characterized the *Suite de Merlin* gives way in the early books of the *Morte D'Arthur* to a simple preoccupation with the thunder of battle, while the mystical orientation of the *Queste del Sanz Graal* is substantially modified in Malory's emphasis upon the *earthly* chivalry of Galahad. It is true that picturesque description of castles and finery was not one of Malory's strong points, but this element was easily added to the Arthurian tradition by the retrospective imagination of later poets; aided by the imagery of the early ballads, they projected into a stylized medieval setting that air of the quaint and curious which seems to surround Malory's style. One finds the result of this process in the early Tennyson, who had (in a sense) imagined the ill-fated mural in the Oxford Union before it was executed by Rossetti and his enthusiastic young disciples. That the epic and picturesque modes had eventually become part of an organic whole may be seen in the closing stanza of Morris' "Golden Wings," which represent a sort of index to the peculiar quality of early Victorian medievalism:

> The draggled swans most eagerly eat
>   The green weeds trailing in the moat;
>   Inside the rotting leaky boat
> You see a slain man's stiffen'd feet.

The Celtic tradition, on the other hand, had stressed the supernatural element in the adventures of ancient heroes, sacrificing the "realism" of conventional human conflict for a sense of wonder and awe at intrusions from beyond the boundaries of the normal and the rational. The merger of this tradition with Romantic supernaturalism in the poems of the *Oisin* volume has already been remarked, as has Yeats' awareness of the basic contrast between the Norse and Irish "tempers." The continuation of his review of Lady Gregory's *Cuchulain of Muirthemne* throws greater illumination upon this contrast and its significance for Yeats' peculiar treatment of antiquity:

We think of actual life when we read those Norse stories, which were already in decadence, so necessary were the proportions of actual life to their efforts, when a dying man remembered his heroism enough to look down at his wound and say, 'Those broad spears are coming into fashion'; but the Irish stories make us understand why the Greeks call myths the activities of the daemons. (*Explorations*, p. 8)

It is precisely this element of the daemonic which is missing from the medieval poems of both Tennyson and the Pre-Raphaelites, and which differentiates those poems from the corresponding efforts of the Romantics, in whose footsteps they considered themselves to be following. Rossetti, to be sure, suggests the daemonic strain in "Sister Helen," but even there the focus is really upon the aborted love affair, the vengeful sweetheart, and the ballad-like entrances of the various "Keiths." One does not sense the ominous impingement of a hostile netherworld upon a Gothic setting, as in Coleridge's "Christabel" where the boundaries of familiar reality are terrifyingly obscured. In general, Rossetti drew from the traditional ballad the standard apparatus of aristocratic love and a wealth of sensuous archaic detail, but neglected the supernatural motifs in which the ballad abounded. No voyages actually take the hero into supernatural realms, as in Keats' "La Belle Dame Sans Merci"; Lord Sands of "Stratton Water" rescues his bride under romantic but natural circumstances and ends the poem a rejoicing lover, unlike the "haggard . . . and . . . woebegone" knight who has gazed upon the forbidden. Thus, in the loss of supernatural energy and in the tendency towards the epical-picturesque veins of medievalism, the Pre-Raphaelites may be viewed in a closer connection with Tennyson than has been commonly supposed to be the case. These changes were all part of an aesthetically legitimate process of humanization which perhaps reached illegitimate lengths in the moralistic allegorical mode of the *Idylls of the King*. Beside this production of the older Tennyson, Pre-Raphaelite poetry indeed acquires an aura of Romantic "purity" which is likely to obscure the fact that this poetry had certain common roots with that of the early Tennyson. It was partly this community of origin which made Tennyson's moralizing of his medieval song a somewhat insidious obstacle to Rossetti and Morris. By compromising the romantic past rather than placing himself firmly in the camp of the enemy, Tennyson had made it probable—as T.E. Welby observes—that poets who did not represent their knights as modern English gentlemen would be accused of "willful perversity" and "insane sensuality." [6]

The case for Yeats as something of an aesthetic *isolato* now becomes clearer. His temperament, his youthful obsession with Shelley, his Celtic heritage—all united to preserve in him that Romantic strain of the daemonic which had otherwise become extinct or passed into a simulacrum of its former state years before his birth. "The Seeker," despite its obvious weaknesses, was perhaps the first poem in the half-century after the death of Coleridge to exhibit an abiding sense of the supernatural as the hostile, ominous arena of man's ultimate endeavors, while "The Wanderings of Oisin," four years later, presents a vision of the nebulous otherworld and its superhuman inhabitants unparalleled in the exotic but concretized and finite medieval world of Rossetti and Morris. When Oisin leaves the familiar lands of the Fenians he enters a realm in which the basic laws of matter and motion, of cause and effect, no longer apply, and the drama is in large part the result of the discrepancy between his humanity and the superhuman conditions to which he is expected to adapt himself.

The uniqueness of "Oisin" is emphasized by a comparison of the poem with Tennyson's treatment of Irish lore in "The Voyage of Maeldune," which had appeared several years earlier. An unfavorable comparison had been made by the *Manchester Guardian* reviewer quoted above, who found that ". . . The chief poem ['The Wanderings of Oisin'] . . . is very unequal.

[6] T.E. Welby, *The Victorian Romantics* (London, 1929), p. 36.

No-one has handled these extraordinary fascinating Irish legends thoroughly well in English verse except the Laureate in his wonderful 'Voyage of Maeldune'." One wonders if anything could be more "unequal" than the line of Tennyson's poem which reads: "And the cock couldn't crow, and the bull couldn't low, and the dog couldn't bark"; but leaving this point aside, the Tennysonian conception of Irish legend appears as a picturesque unfolding of exotica, completely lacking in the daemonic elements which inform "Oisin." Maeldune visits a series of islands, such as the Isle of Flowers, the Isle of Fruits, and the Isle of Fire, but the sequence has little more significance than that of an unusual travelogue. The mode is closer to the bizarre kaleidoscopic catalogue of the poet's early "Recollections of the Arabian Nights" than it is to the Romantic preoccupation with the spiritual ontology of myth.

If the twenty-year-old Yeats was not, then, "in all things pre-Raphaelite," it remains to determine in what things he was. At least two legitimate applications of the term suggest themselves, both related to the peculiar circumstances of Yeats' life and aesthetic milieu, and in particular to the influence of his father. In the first place, "Pre-Raphaelite" made a convenient comprehensive term for any poetry opposed in its sensuousness, stylistic emphasis, and exotic subject matter to the poetry of moralization and didacticism associated with Tennyson, Arnold, and company. This sense of the word is clearly associated with Yeats' contention in "Art and Ideas" that:

> . . . the turning of Rossetti to religious themes, his dislike of Wordsworth were but the one impulse, for he more than any other was in reaction against the period of philanthropy and reform that created the pedantic composure of Wordsworth, the rhetoric of Swinburne, the passionless sentiment of Tennyson. (EI, pp. 351–352)

With the addition of the swaggering tag "in all things" one has the ideal rallying cry against the Philistine enemy as he was viewed by his younger colleagues. Secondly, Pre-Raphaelite emphasis upon the connection between poetry and the visual arts reached Yeats through his own immersion in a world of painters in his early years. The circle of artists who worked in the vicinity of Bedford Park may have begun to find fault with the work of Rossetti, but they made no secret of the fact that he had been their original touchstone and inspiration. Certainly his influence remains strong enough to exert its effect upon Yeats the art student, who longed for "pattern, for pre-Raphaelitism, for an art allied to poetry" (A, p. 49).

Yeats had, of course, received the Pre-Raphaelite gospel directly through his father. One reminiscence in "Reveries" is particularly revealing:

> He [J.B. Yeats] disliked the Victorian poetry of ideas, and Wordsworth but for certain passages of whole poems. He said one morning over his breakfast that he had discovered in the shape of a Wordsworthian scholar, an old and greatly respected clergyman whose portrait he was painting, all the animal instincts of a prizefighter. He despised the formal beauty of Raphael, that calm which is not an ordered passion but an hypocrisy, and attacked Raphael's life for its love of pleasure and its self-indulgence. In literature he was always pre-Raphaelite, and carried into literature principles that, while the Academy was still unbroken, had made the first attack upon academic form. (A, p. 40)

The implicit analogy here between "the Victorian poetry of ideas" and "the formal beauty of Raphael" should not go unnoticed. Both may be seen as laden with conventions which constitute barriers to the purer and more intense forms of aesthetic experience, but it is difficult to go beyond this rather general comparison to specific equations. No doubt J.B. Yeats was aware of the Pre-Raphaelites' distaste for gray tones, and their emphasis upon "truth to nature" in the background while the foreground was occupied by romantic subjects from mythology and scripture; but these were hardly the sort of "principles" which could be carried over into literature, unless one either generalized them considerably or chose to make one's poems descriptions of paintings. The first course suggests the "rallying-cry" aspect of Pre-Raphaelitism which the son sensed in the father's colorful, polemic conversation; the second, certain features of Yeats' early work which seem the direct result of an interest in Pre-Raphaelite painting and that portion of Pre-Raphaelite poetry which imitated painting.

In this latter connection at least two of Yeats' early uncollected poems seem to have some relaton to the Rossettian genre of "sonnets on pictures," in which paintings are described as unfolding action, usually in the present tense, while abstract emotional qualities and explanations of symbolic significance are interpolated among the visualized physical details. The sonnet "For a Marriage of St. Catherine by Hans Memmelinck" is representative of Rossetti's work in this medium:

> MYSTERY: Catherine the bride of Christ.
> She kneels, and on her hand the holy Child
> Now sets the ring. Her life is hushed and mild,
> Laid in God's knowledge—ever unenticed
> From God, and in the end thus fitly priced.
> Awe, and the music that is near her, wrought
> Of angels, have possessed her eyes in thought:
> Her utter joy is hers, and hath sufficed.
>
> There is a pause while Mary Virgin turns
> The leaf, and reads. With eyes on the spread book
> That damsel at her knees reads after her.
> John whom He loved, and John His harbinger,
> Listen and watch. Whereon soe'er thou look,
> The light is starred in gems and the gold burns. (*Poems*, II)

Here the attitudes of the divine celebrants are described with a simplicity approaching naïveté, and physical description merges easily into the metaphysical province which the painter could only suggest as Rossetti expounds the religious symbolism of the grouping. The second stanza marks a return to literal portrayal, but it too flowers into the suggestion of blinding cosmic significance immanent in a humble, pietistic group with the closing line: "The light is starred in gems and the gold burns."

The poem of Yeats which belongs most obviously to the same genre is entitled "On Mr. Nettleship's Picture at the Royal Hibernian Academy," and here the link with Rossetti is reinforced by the identity of the artist. John Trivett Nettleship, a member of the artistic circle with which J.B. Yeats was associated when in London, was among those "who had been influenced by the Pre-Raphaelite movement but had lost their confidence." Nettleship in especial had had close ties with the master, as Yeats recalls in the same passage of the *Autobiographies*: " ... though Nettleship had already turned lion painter, my father talked constantly of the designs of his youth, especially of 'God creating Evil,' which Rossetti praised in a letter my father had seen 'as the most sublime conception in ancient or modern Art.' " The painting described by Yeats' poem is obviously from the period when Nettleship "had already turned lion painter":

> Yonder the sickle of the moon sails on,
> But here the Lioness licks her soft cub
> Tender and fearless on her funeral pyre:
> Above, saliva dripping from his jaws,
> The Lion, the world's great solitary, bends
> Lowly the head of his magnificence
> And roars, mad with the touch of the unknown,
> Not as he shakes the forest; but a cry
> Low, long and musical. A dew-drop hung
> Bright on a grass blade's under side, might hear,
> Nor tremble to its fall. The fire sweeps round
> Re-shining in his eyes. So ever moves
> The flaming circle of the outer Law,
> Nor heeds the old, dim protest and the cry
> The orb of the most inner living heart
> Gives forth. He, the Eternal, works His will.

Here again we have simple description interlarded with comment on emotional states—"Tender and fearless," for example—and interpretation of symbolism—"So ever moves / The flaming circle of the outer Law." As in Rossetti's sonnets, the succession of present-tense factual statements gives to the unfolding action a static, inflexible quality which aptly suggests painting.

When no such suggestion is intended, however, this rigidity can be a positive barrier to the flow of narrative, and it is likely that much of Yeats' earlier-mentioned difficulty with settings in the "cloud-and-foam" period is the result of moving from the wish for "an art allied to poetry" to a poetry allied to art. It is significant in this connection that the poem just quoted appeared during this period, which saw the awkward backdrop painting of "The Two Titans" and "Ferencz Renyi." The stasis induced by this sort of painter's visualization may be sensed, in fact, throughout Yeats' verse of the late Eighties, even when extended descriptive passages are not present, and it undoubtedly accounts for many of the "tapestry-like" effects noted by Ellmann and others.[7]

Another poem of Yeats which seems to imitate a Pre-Raphaelite painting is "She Dwelt among the Sycamores," mentioned above in connection with the difficulties of narrational transition which beset Yeats for a time. Here it is the insistence upon "precision" of coloring and number, and upon a microscopic focus in general which marks the tell-tale Pre-Raphaelite objective of "truth to nature." The single "ash-gray feather"; the "six feet / Lapped in the lemon daffodils"; the "four eyes"—all these represent the practice of artistic principles which began with the "seven" stars of the Blessed Damozel's crown and reached as far as the "nine bean rows" of the Lake Isle.

Such extended experiments in word-painting were part of a rather ephemeral phase of Yeats' early apprenticeship; a more

[7] See *Identity*, p. 38.

permanent influence of Pre-Raphaelite art on the young poet may be seen in his preoccupation with a type of womanhood realized in the paintings of Burne-Jones and Rossetti, and with the gestures, attitudes, and expressions inherent in the tragic poetic isolation which the type suggested. Here, as in the case of the "Oisin" statues, we approach Yeats' concern with certain "types" as the ideal characterless personae of tragedy, in opposition to the sub-tragic "individual." Yeats ties Pre-Raphaelite woman specifically to this concept in "The Death of Synge":

> The old art, if carried to its logical conclusion, would have led to the creation of one single type of man, one single type of woman; gathering up by a kind of deification a capacity for all energy and all passion, into a Krishna, a Christ, a Dionysius; and at times a poetical painter, a Botticelli, a Rossetti, creates as his supreme achievement one type of face, known afterwards by his name. (A, p. 304)

Grossman, in an extended and enlightening discussion of the Yeatsian women in *The Wind Among the Reeds*, ties them specifically to the "White Woman" of the European Wisdom tradition; but he does not dwell upon the Rossettian prototypes which lay so much closer to hand for Yeats during the Eighties and Nineties.

The face was a composite of the features of Jane Burden and Elizabeth Siddal—the long aristocratic nose, the "dream-heavy" eyelids, the swan-neck, the thick flowing hair—and was visible to Yeats in numerous paintings which he had the opportunity to study at length in London and Liverpool. It was also abundantly visible in Pre-Raphaelite poetry, representing in general the most striking common feature of art and verse in a movement renowned for embracing both. Rossetti and Morris placed heavy emphasis upon capturing the significant details of posture and expression in their heroines, since the whole structure of aesthetic values in their verse was dependent upon conveying an impression of the mixture of languishing unearthly nobility, exalted ritualistic demeanor, and mysterious sadness which surrounded the phenomenon of woman's beauty. The Blessed Damozel with eyes "deeper than the depth / Of waters stilled at even" and hair "yellow like ripe corn"; the Queen of "Staff and Scrip" gazing "sadly" up from her loom amid odors of "musk and myrrh"; the beloved model of "The Portrait," whose face is shrined "Mid mystic trees where light falls in / Hardly at all. . . ."—all of these represent a poetry in which mere pose has acquired poetic significance far beyond the customary. In "The Haystack in the Floods" Morris furnishes an extended example of precise description of attitude:

> She rode astride as troopers do;
> With kirtle kilted to her knee,
> To which the mud splash'd wretchedly;
> And the wet dripped from every tree
> Upon her head and heavy hair,
> And on her eyelids broad and fair. . . .

Though the impression here is one of noble beauty subjected to rough treatment, Morris does not allow the impression of nobility to flag.

Yeats exhibits the influence of the Pre-Raphaelite conception of woman as early as *The Island of Statues*, where the Enchantress describes Naschina's hair as "Long citron coils that have about thee blown / In shadowy dimness." In keeping with his affinity for the daemonic, Yeats exploits the sense of the ominous in such beauty more than had his predecessors, rising to the extravagant in the well-known description of Niamh from "The Wanderings of Oisin":

> And like a sunset were her lips,
> A stormy sunset o'er doomed ships.

Ellmann complains that this description, evocative as it is, seems better suited to one of Rossetti's women than to Oisin's lady, but the aura of impending doom is even stronger than in most Rossettian similes, and is not really inappropriate to the scene in which Oisin makes the tragic decision to abandon his mortality. The rest of the portrait, however, with its "silver cinctures" and "white vesture," is strictly in keeping with the decorativeness of "a Rossetti or Burne-Jones painting" (*Masks*, p. 52).

By the appearance of The Celtic Twilight in 1893 these exotic details of dress are giving way to a more powerful and abstract conception of feminine pose, the significance of which will be examined later, but it is relevant to note here that the outline is still unmistakably Pre-Raphaelite. The Rose of the World is distinguished by "red lips, with all their mournful pride," and by a "lonely face" on which lives "foam of the sky." [8] Six years later the heroines of *The Wind Among the Reeds* invariably appear with "Passion-dimmed eyes and long heavy hair," and the women whose prayers Red Hanrahan requests are envisaged in a typically Rossettian ritual attitude: ". . . Colleens kneeling by your altar-rails. . . ." [9]

If Yeats had found in the Pre-Raphaelites a traditional basis for "pure" poetry, he found contemporary encouragement for this poetry in the Rhymers' Club, who met weekly at the Cheshire Cheese in London. That there were certain strands of continuity between the two groups is made obvious by Yeats' memoir of "The Tragic Generation":

> Woman herself was still in our eyes romantic and mysterious, still the priestess of our shrine, our emotions remembering the *Lilith* and *Sybilla Palmifera* of Rossetti; for as yet the sense of comedy, which was soon to mould the very fashion plates; and, in the eyes of men of my generation, to destroy at last the sense of beauty itself, had scarce begun to show here and there, in slight subordinate touches among the designs of great painters and craftsmen. It could not be otherwise, for Johnson's favorite phrase, that life is ritual, expressed something that was in some

[8] "The Rose of the World."
[9] "He reproves the Curlew" and "The Lover speaks to the Hearers of his Songs in Coming Days."

degree in all our thoughts, and how could life be ritual if woman had not her symbolical place. (A, p. 181)

Yeats furnishes us here with a valuable insight into the central aesthetic of the Rhymers, an aesthetic in which the ceremony of the Rossettian "cult of the woman" is seen as part of a much larger religious ceremony of life, marked by pontifical solemnity and the manipulation of sacred symbols. Graham Hough sees the moving spirit of Rossetti, not entirely benign, behind the larger ceremony as well:

> The significance of Rossetti's work for the sensibility of the *fin-de-siècle* is very great. It inaugurates that period of emotional unrest in which satisfaction is sought in the traditional religious symbolism, but is not found, since the symbols have been emptied of almost all their traditional religious content. We begin to discern for the first time the figure of the conscious aesthete, deliberately pursuing beauty. . . .[10]

Hough is perhaps a little too upset that Rossetti lacks the scholastic complexity and sincere medieval faith of Dante, but one could hardly question his implication that the *fin-de-siècle* poets—which in England meant more or less the Rhymers—pushed to its logical conclusion the Rossettian exploitation of the aesthetic side of Catholic ritual and doctrine. Many of Lionel Johnson's poems seem intended to make of life not simply a ritual but a formal Mass, in which all noisy, commonplace activities of life die into the majestic, ordered serenity of the Divine Presence. Thus two dead lovers are remembered in "Trentals":

> Gray without, the autumn air:
> But pale candles here prepare,
> Pale as wasted golden hair.
> Let the quire with mourning descant
> Cry: *In pace requiescat!*

Of all Rhymers, it is Johnson who comes closest to Yeats

[10] Graham Hough, *The Last Romantics* (London, 1949), p. 81.

in ritualistic imagery. He frequently exhibits a concern with the portrayal of the spiritual qualities of celestial beings, suggesting the diaphanous, flame-like nature of a higher Platonic reality. More importantly, Johnson is also occupied with the religious awe inherent in a consideration of universals. At times he seems to rise to an almost Shelleyan intensity of vision, a plateau on which an apocalyptic upheaval of the cosmic structure is made to seem possible, but he inevitably recedes into the serene, decorative religiosity which had been Rossetti's legacy. Such is the pattern of movement in the opening of "St. Columba," where the crescendo of the first stanza quickly gives way to diminuendo in the second:

> Dead is Columba: the world's arch
> Gleams with a lightning of strange fires.
> They flash and run, they leap and march,
> Signs of a Saint's fulfilled desires.
> Live is Columba; golden crowned,
> Sceptered with Mary lilies, shod
> With angel flames, and girdled round
> With white of snow, he goes to God.

It seems probable that Johnson's obsession with the Catholic aesthetic left its influence on Yeats during their friendship of the Nineties. Certainly there had been no "grey clouds of incense," "candles at Mother Mary's feet," "altar rails," or "wounds in palm and side" in Yeats' non-Christian upbringing. He owed this part of his eclectic religion mainly to the Catholicism in which the Rhymers sought artistic and spiritual succor, although there were vivid adaptations of Christianity in the Golden Dawn ritual, as Virginia Moore points out in her fascinating description of the symbolic "crucifixion" which Yeats underwent as part of his initiation into this arcane society.[11]

Johnson's use of the invocation, an obvious dramatic mode of religious poetry, also parallels the practice of Yeats, though

[11] Virginia Moore, *The Unicorn* (New York, 1954), pp. 149–150.

the parallel fails to extend to the complexity and intensity of the latter's invocations. The appeal to Yeats' desire for "heroic" speech is obvious; since man is addressing superior powers his speech is of necessity cast on an exalted plane, though this exaltation may in fact become tiresomely pontifical. Both invocation and preoccupation with awesome elementals are exhibited in a series of quatrains which Johnson entitles "The Red Wind." A representative stanza runs:

> Wind of the East! Red Wind!
> Thou witherest the soft breath
> Of Paradise the kind:
> Red Wind of burning death!

That Yeats shares an obvious community of method with this author become obvious when we read in his poem "The Unappeasable Host":

> Desolate winds that cry over the wandering sea;
> Desolate winds that hover in the flaming West;
> Desolate winds that beat the doors of Heaven, and beat
> The doors of Hell.

The sense of ritual is also strong in Ernest Dowson, who had been converted to Catholicism while at Oxford, but his ritualistic imagery lacks the cosmic spiritual dimension which is sometimes present in the poetry of Johnson, and which permeates the poetry of Yeats. The sacred, mysterious ceremonies of the church call him to rest from a riotous round of "decadent" activities rather than to a position in the flux and brilliance of the divine fire. "Without," says Dowson, "the sullen noises of the street"; but within:

> Dark is the church, and dim the worshippers,
>   Hushed with bowed heads as though by some old spell,
> While through the incense-laden air there stirs
>   The admonition of a silver bell.[12]

[12] *The Poems of Ernest Dowson*, ed. Longaker (Philadelphia, 1962). All subsequent citations of Dowson are to this edition.

He is particularly fascinated by the serene, cloistered life of religious orders, but here again his fascination is with the peculiarly human compensations of such a life. His poems "Nuns of the Perpetual Adoration" and "Carthusians" both express the familiar *fin-de-siècle* longing to enjoy relief from the "loud" and "passionate" behind "austere walls" where "no voices penetrate," and both express an envy of those who experience no unsettling changes of mood and mind:

> And it is one with them when evening falls,
> And one with them the cold return of day. . . .

This religiosity was, for the Rhymers, a mode of artistic purity antithetical to the moralization of their older contemporaries, but the shadow of Tennyson extended as subtly and inexorably to their endeavors as it had to those of the Pre-Raphaelites. The dilemma of man in an infinite universe; the dilemma of man in the throes of religious doubt; the dilemma of man torn between hedonism and divine duty—all of these appeared, in the familiar styles involving various blends of the discursive and the aphoristic, in the two anthologies of the Rhymers' Club, published in 1892 and 1894. In the opening lines of G. A. Greene's "Beyond," for instance, we have a strong reminiscence of Tennyson's "Vastness," complete with the air of scientific speculation and earthbound uncertainty:

> What lies beyond the splendour of the sun,
> Beyond his flashing belt of sister-spheres?
> What deeps are they whereinto disappears
> The visitant comet's sword of fire fine-spun.[13]

In a line from "The Pathfinder" reminiscent of Clough, the same poet points out that it does not matter if the toiler has achieved nothing, "Because to aspire is better than to attain."

Even Lionel Johnson's poetry exhibits traces of the influence it was designed to counteract. Some of the epigrammatic

[13] *The Book of the Rhymers' Club* (London, 1894).

quatrains of "The Dark Angel" seem modelled stylistically upon *In Memoriam*, while "A Burden of Easter Vigil" echoes the quaverings of faith in that same Tennyson poem in the familiar tone of anguished skepticism:

> Awhile meet Doubt and Faith:
> For either sigheth and saith,
>   That he is dead. . . .
> . . . .
> He loved us all: is dead;
>   May rise again.
>   *But if he rise not?*

In the examples quoted above, Tennyson's aesthetic merely intrudes upon the poetry of the Rhymers; in the tension between hedonism and the religious life, however, it surrounds this poetry in an atmosphere of specifically moralistic concern which is no less moralistic for its coming down on the side of the daringly immoral. The position of the persona who admitted the vacuity of the purely aesthetic life in "The Palace of Art" gives way to that of one who alternates between sad revelling in his damnation as a hedonist-aesthete and wistful looks at the contentment of some religious haven. However changed the role of the sinner, the Rhymers are still obsessed with sin and salvation, and thus disobey Yeats' ironically contemporary admonition in the poem "Into the Twilight": "Come clear of the nets of wrong and right."

These "nets" had, of course, been successfully negotiated at times by many earlier poets, Tennyson among them; moral choice was by no means an illegitimate arena for poetry. The real shortcoming of the Rhymers' verse, from a later-Yeatsian standpoint, was in the atmosphere of indecisive wavering which surrounded the dilemma of the persona. The cathedral and the monastery are there as refuges, but those inside celebrating the ritual are seldom the poets. These latter neither renounce their "sinful" lives nor embrace them with defiant enthusiasm; as a result, the notion of an escape into the sanctum frequently acquires an aura of dilettantish toying and idle speculation rather than gives an impression of the tragic crossroads reached.

The deeper roots of this sense of weakness and equivocation lay in the relentless introspection of what Yeats called "the gentle, sensitive mind," a phenomenon which he saw as the aesthetic cross of most post-Shakespearian generations, and particularly of his own:

> *Hic.* . . . I would find myself and not an image.
> *Ille.* That is our modern hope, and by its light
> We have lit upon the gentle, sensitive mind
> And lost the old nonchalance of the hand.
> ("Ego Dominus Tuus")

Dowson and Johnson were giving an accurate portrayal of the contemporary aesthete's spiritual perplexity and inability to act decisively, but honesty is not always the best dramatic policy. Though the situations which they present appear quite realistic beside Yeats' wholehearted poetical acceptance of a fantastic eclectic religion, this very "realism" meant that they had fallen into at least the outer reaches of the psychological web spun earlier by Tennyson and Arnold.

This web was centered upon modern man, intelligent and sensitive but spiritually debilitated and morally uncertain. One may trace its beginnings back to an attempt to resurrect the Romantic hero in an age when the resurrectors themselves had been strongly attracted to the antithetical life represented by bourgeois respectability and the functioning of stern moral imperatives such as the call to "duty." The Victorian counterparts of Manfred and Alastor no longer spurned human society in favor of solitary daemonic pursuits; instead, they debated the merits of various escapes from oppressive conventionality and ended up in vacillation, choosing none. Romantic *angst*, in some degree, was still a driving force but it was

mitigated by the process of weighing and balancing alternatives, a process which may exhibit the delicate discriminatory
functioning of the highly developed mind in the real world,
yet is likely to lead in poetry to a sense of equivocation and
unheroic passivity.

Thus, although Tennyson's early heroes dream of retreat-
ing into an anti-social life of art, they are unable to cast off
the guilt attached to neglecting what they have been taught
to regard as moral obligations. The Palace of Art, with its
arrogant atmosphere of "God-like isolation," is made unin-
habitable by the soul's qualms over her lack of social involvement, and the sensuous escapism of "The Lotus-Eaters" must
be perceived against a background of moral condemnation
for those willing to forget the "confusion" of their homeland
and "Let what is broken so remain." A more thorough ana-
tomization of "the gentle, sensitive mind" is found in the
psychological portrait of the "Locksley Hall" persona, whose
"palsied heart" and "jaundiced eye" suggest a febrile morbidity rather than the mode of the mysteriously saturnine.
Visited by a succession of exhilarating memories and impulses
of escape to some mindless tropical paradise, he seems doomed
to dissipate his energies in a psychological conflict equivalent
to futility and inaction in the objective world of men. The
optimistic departure with which the poem closes is unconvincing; the air of circling ratiocination stifles any attempt to
evoke the impression of heroic decision.

This air becomes even stronger in the aesthete-hero portrayed by Matthew Arnold. The focus is no longer upon
neurotic morbidity but upon the agony of indecision itself,
and the perspective of the speaker upon his own problem
puts us at yet another remove from the spontaneity and im-
pulsiveness of the active man. More obviously than in Tennyson's poetry the persona is the poet himself, ruminating upon
the tension between the desire to embrace a brooding solitude,
and the sense of social consciousness partially inculcated at

Rugby. The loss of religious faith is another factor which adds to the atmosphere of sad perplexity, and again we find the mind circling about among many alternatives, ravenous for a sense of commitment and yet doubting the absolute value of any given heroic act:

> What helps it now, that Byron bore
> With haughty scorn which mock'd the smart,
> Through Europe to the Aetolian shore
> The pageant of this bleeding heart? [14]

These lines are in "Stanzas from the Grande Chartreuse," a poem of particular significance for our study since one of the alternatives which Arnold is considering is the monastic life of the Carthusians, a path of escape from agonizing restlessness which later occurred to Dowson in the lyric "Carthusians." Both poets are struck by the ghostly austerity and silent isolation of the monks' existence, and see in this existence something of an antidote for their respective forms of *Weltschmerz*; and, most significantly, both fail to embrace that way of life, Arnold returning to his position amidst intellectual contrarieties and Dowson to his halfhearted immersion in the rose-flinging throng.

There are, of course, differences which the two poets themselves would have stressed if presented with the opportunity for a comparison of their respective works. Arnold's poem has a much more obvious atmosphere of ethical ratiocination than Dowson's—an atmosphere which stems largely from the poet's perspective on his own position as the hesitant questioner. The extent of this perspective may be judged from the famous preface to his poems of 1853, in which he rejects "Empedocles on Etna" for reasons which would also condemn "Grande Chartreuse" if one were to apply the standards of tragic drama to lyric poetry, as Yeats later did:

[14] Matthew Arnold, *Poetry and Prose* (Cambridge, Mass., 1954).

What then are the situations, from the representation of which, though accurate, no poetical enjoyment can be derived? They are those in which the suffering finds no vent in action; in which a continuous state of mental distress is prolonged, unrelieved by incident, hope, or resistance; in which there is everything to be endured, nothing to be done. In such situations there is inevitably something morbid, in the description of them something monotonous. When they occur in actual life, they are painful, not tragic; the representation of them in poetry is painful also.[15]

Arnold had sensed the danger of excessive skepticism and its resultant passivity several years before when he mitigated his friendship with Clough for fear that the latter's extreme analytic and critical bias would contaminate the springs of poetry in his acquaintances; but Arnold was unable to escape some of the same effects from his own temperament.

Dowson lacked this perspective, but prided himself on being free of the moralization and general discursiveness which marred Victorian poetry as far as the Rhymers were concerned. However, although his "Carthusians" achieves a greater degree of lyric "purity" than Arnold's poem, and places the persona in a more romantic position by making him a doomed reveller, this persona does not escape the aura of "passive suffering" which had hung over almost every contemplative hero of the previous fifty years. The wildness is as unconvincing as the optimism which closed "Locksley Hall," and the prevailing impression is that of the delicate, aesthetic temperament displaying its "nerves in patterns on a screen" as it vacillates between dreams of sensual abandonment and yet other dreams of a death-like calm. Johnson, despite the greater energy of his religious images, frequently portrays the same temperament. One has only to read "To a Passionist" to discover a parallel situation in which the poet envies the initiates, and a parallel display of querulous uncertainty:

[15] "Poetry and the Classics," *Selections from the Prose Works of Matthew Arnold*, ed. W. S. Johnson (Cambridge, Mass., 1913), p. 3.

Canst thou be right? Is thine the very truth?
Stands then our life in so forlorn a state?
Nay, but thou wrongest us: thou wrong'st our youth,
Who dost our happiness compassionate.
And yet! and yet! O royal Calvary!

Considerations such as those above lead me to wonder whether Bloom does not somewhat overvalue Johnson's "The Dark Angel." He succeeds in showing that there is a powerful conflict immanent in the poem's conceptualization, but not that the conflict is artistically realized with such completeness that the work "... is much the best poem written in English during the Nineties." (Bloom, p. 46) Certainly one finds in it daemonic encounter of a more vivid variety than is usual in the poetry of the Rhymers, and a concluding note of defiance based on what Bloom terms "the unmixed spirituality of Newman." (Bloom, p. 49) But spirituality in the passive form of abstention is hardly the stuff of heroic drama, and the prevailing impression of the poem is one of Johnson as "gentle, sensitive" victim rather than autonomous defier of the dark powers. The rhetorical staleness of such phrases as "flames of evil ecstasy" presents yet another problem with regard to Bloom's claims for the poem, but one best considered in light of a later discussion of the Rhymers' diction and syntax.

Dowson's and Johnson's belief that they had escaped the tentacles of Victorianism by eschewing the more obvious characteristics of the ethical essay was but a special case of a general error of the Nineties. Years later, Yeats, the only Rhymer of note who lived long enough to acquire perspective, analyzed the case incisively in his introduction to the *Oxford Book of Modern Verse*:

> When my generation denounced scientific humanitarian preoccupation, psychological curiosity, rhetoric, we had not found what ailed Victorian literature. The Elizabethans had all these things, especially rhetoric. ... The mischief began at the end of the seventeenth century when man became passive before a

mechanized nature; that lasted to our own day with the exception of a brief period between Smart's *Song to David* and the death of Byron, wherein imprisoned man beat upon the door. (p. xxvii)

The analysis itself, must, of course, be placed in another kind of perspective; the word "ailed" bespeaks Yeats' impatient dismissal of all "passive" subjects as unsuited to poetry, and points towards his insistence upon applying the standards of tragedy to the lyric. Although such a limitation proved highly felicitous in the case of his own works, it obviously represents an eccentric and autocratic dictum which excludes most Neoclassical, Victorian, and modern poetry from the body of respectability. The infamous omission of Wilfred Owens' war poetry from the anthology on the one hand, and the elevation of Oliver St. John Gogarty to the position of "one of the great lyric poets of our age" (p. xv) on the other, are corollaries which tend to undermine the general validity of the original theorem.

Nonetheless, despite these objections, Yeats' analysis is the result of a mature attitude which was already nascent in the Nineties, and was already differentiating his aesthetic from those of the other Rhymers. Granted, the early Yeatsian personae appeared at times to hover in gentle sensitivity among clouds of incense; they also exhibited heroic involvement in the mysteries of a Rossettian religion of love which, however eclectic and artificial it may seem, placed its adherents on the boundary of the supernatural—a level on which tragic elevation and tragic intensity always became possible for Yeats. Yielding fully to the religious commitment which Dowson and Johnson admitted was beyond their grasp, these personae occupied themselves in direct encounter with cosmic forces which were, in Yeats' mind, mysteriously related to feminine beauty.

That all of this amounted, actually, to yet another mode of the daemonic is emphasized by the reappearance of the symbolic figures from the Demogorgon complex in a new connection with "Beauty":

> . . . flame on flame, deep under deep,
> Throne over throne where in half sleep
> Their swords upon their iron knees
> Brood her high lonely mysteries.[16]

Yeats found in the daemonic a valuable isolation from what Wallace Stevens has called "the pressure of reality," though this isolation was perhaps more extreme than any envisaged by Stevens; it extended, after all, to an avoidance of the emotional conflicts inherent in the actual and immediate circumstances of the poet's life. By facing these conflicts and admitting the dilemma of the gentle, sensitive mind, Dowson and Johnson had come closer than Yeats to dealing with the human realities for which poetry is ultimately responsible, but they had been thrown into the arena before their powers of expression were mature; the result was the poverty of fresh linguistic conception noted by Hough and others.[17] Yeats, on the other hand, chose to develop these powers in an imaginary realm of manufactured elevation and intensity, and later brought them to bear upon the verities of contemporary life. The personae of this world, moreover, were not reflections of the poet's doubt and perplexity, but represented early forms of the Yeatsian mask in their positive stance as active initiates of a mysterious cult.

The synthesized eclectic religion which provided Yeats' framework in the Nineties drew heavily from Rossetti on the one hand, and heavily from Yeats' immersion in arcana on the other. Woman, of course, was the center, and her Dantesque transfiguration into a reflection of divinity in Rossetti's *The House of Life* represents the closest Victorian parallel to Yeats' idealization. Certainly the deference accorded Dowson's Cynara, and, slightly earlier, Morris' Guinevere, does not approach the religious awe with which both Rossetti and Yeats treat the female figures at the centers of their respective cults. Man's destiny becomes, for both poets, largely dependent upon his

---

[16] "He remembers Forgotten Beauty."
[17] See especially *The Last Romantics*, pp. 212–214.

attitude and actions in the service of this goddess incarnate, who is connected with a complex of mysterious ultimate forces. Those who enter the sanctum are permitted to transcend mortal limitations and to commune somehow with the infinite; such is the case in Rossetti's sonnet XXXV, "The Dark Glass":

> Lo! what am I to Love, the lord of all?
>> One murmuring shell he gathers from the sand—
>> One little heart-flame sheltered in his hand.
> Yet through thine eyes he grants me clearest call
> And veriest touch of powers primordial
>> That any hour-girt life may understand. (*Poems*, II)

Nonetheless, though Yeats found warrant for the cult of "Love" in *The House of Life*, his mode of religiosity is quite different from that of Rossetti and, one may venture to say, more effective dramatically. Rossetti lacks a coherent and clearly-visualized body of images through which to express the supernatural aspects of love, and he tends to fall back upon a thinly realized version of the machinery of Dantesque allegory. The impression of thinness is increased by the fact that, as Graham Hough points out, the images do not have the theological correspondants which they had in Dante; they represent an attempt to turn an "all too human conception of love" into the highest reality.[18] Ellmann, too, mentions Rossetti's difficulty in "controlling the slide from physical to spiritual." [19] It is not hard to find lines in which spiritual images seem ready Petrarchan superlatives rather than markers of elevation in a seriously-considered Neoplatonic hierarchy—the soul of the woman hidden by "Heaven's own screen," for instance, or her "enthroning throat" above which "Her face is made her shrine." [20] The roles of supernatural personae are filled by dim personifications usually described as "winged," and existing in the ontological limbo of the allegorical. These considerations help explain why

[18] *Ibid.*, p. 80.
[19] *Identity*, p. 75.
[20] See, respectively, Sonnet LVII and Sonnet XI, *Poems* II.

Bloom's assertion that "diction and syntax in early Yeats owe more . . . to Rossetti than to Shelley, let alone to Blake . . ." (p. 106) no longer applies by the Nineties.

Rossetti's difficulty with imagery is part of a larger poverty of fresh diction which afflicted the late nineteenth century. The prevailing poetic language was a currency too common to support a rise into the intensity and new dimensions of the supernatural, as is readily evident from Lionel Johnson's failure to sustain his visualizations of the Christian spiritual order. Yeats, however, was singularly fortunate in this regard, for he had access not only to the relatively unexploited machinery of Celtic myth, but to the apparatus and ceremony of various arcane societies. His involvement with the spiritualistic fringe groups of London in the Nineties has received much derisive comment, but they were an important source of personae, symbols, imagery and diction which had poetic value far beyond their somewhat specious function as actual spiritual realities. Specific debts aside, however, the mere situation of the magical ritual, in which the initiate invokes the ethereal and sometimes ominous powers of the air, worked to enhance Yeats' natural awareness of the drama inherent in the confrontation of the human and superhuman. Furthermore, those elementals of air, water, and fire which had been the core of the Shelleyan cosmic vision were present in new and suggestive combinations in the ceremonial incantations of the Golden Dawn and various other cabalistic orders. Again, it was no doubt the power ascribed to "words alone" in these incantations which encouraged Yeats in the use of the symbol, but this is a topic for the succeeding chapter.

In her valuable study of Yeats' occult activities, Virginia Moore lists several examples of his images of the Nineties which come directly from arcane ritual—the Cabalistic Tree of Life in "The Two Trees"; "the flaming door" from "The Valley of the Black Pig"; the "banners of East and West" from "He hears the Cry of the Sedge"; and others. She concludes, however, that "[during] the decade following 1890, when he joined the Order [of the Golden Dawn], one finds only faint traces of the doctrine and symbols of what he considered to be profound esoteric experiences." [21]

It would appear that Miss Moore's focus here upon Yeats' philosophical activities in general, and upon the intricate actualities of the Golden Dawn ritual in particular, cause her to underestimate the pervading aesthetic influence of such orders upon Yeats' poetry. At the point in the initiation, for instance, when "the blindfold was lifted for a moment to disclose the Hierus as Guardian of the West threatening with his sword," the candidate Yeats was admonished to be without fear, "for he who trembles at the Flame and the Flood and at the Shadows of the Air hath no part in God." [22] Miss Moore merely notes that "the Flame and the Flood" would turn up as a phrase in one of Yeats' poems; the total impact of this portion of the ceremony, however, is considerably greater, as we may judge from an examination of the poem "To his Heart, bidding it have no Fear":

> Be you still, be you still, trembling heart;
> Remember the wisdom out of the old days:
> "Him who trembles before the flame and the flood,"
> And the winds that blow through the starry ways,
> Let the starry winds and the flame and the flood
> Cover over and hide, for he has no part
> With the lonely, majestical multitude.

The very fabric of the poem is a dramatization of a merely human consciousness facing the presence of the ominously superhuman, and as such is the generalized instance of the initiation itself, in which the Hierus had bidden Yeats to "have no Fear." The consequences of fear are also similar—exclusion from "a part in God" on the one hand, and from "the lonely, majestical multitude" on the other. Even the phrasing of the dictum "Him

[21] Moore, p. 179.
[22] Moore, p. 136.

who trembles . . ." is almost synonymous with that of the ritual, the principal difference lying in Yeats' typical enhancement of the dangers involved in the confrontation.

The spiritual animation of the universe, noted in Yeats' earliest Shelleyan verses, received powerful impetus from his involvement with arcane societies. "The Shadows of the Air," as the Golden Dawn ritual calls them, furnished *dramatis personae* far more suited to the cosmic arena than the unfortunate fairies who flit through Yeats' poetry of the late Eighties. In phrases such as "the hovering, piteous, penitential throng"; "sweet everlasting Voices"; and "the guards of the heavenly fold," Yeats was able to capture a positive sense of the ominous and the preternaturally formidable without resorting to concrete embodiments which so limited the sense of spirituality. It all amounted to a dramatically effective blend of the visually vague and the heroically definite: personae which somehow functioned on the tragic plane, but lacked the corporeality through which tragedy is usually perceived. That many of these personae were inspired by arcane societies, and in particular those of Irish druidical connections, is obvious from poems such as "The Poet pleads with the Elemental Powers," which appeared in the first *Book of the Rhymers' Club* under the title "A mystical Prayer to the Masters of the Elements, Finvarra, Feacra, and Caolte." The second stanza not only demonstrates supernatural vocatives at least inspired by those of the magical orders, but is cast in the form of an initiate's prayer:

> Great elemental Powers of wind, and wave, and fire,
> With your harmonious quire,
> Encircle her I love and sing her unto peace,
> That my old care may cease,
> And she forget the wandering and the crimson gloom
> Of the Rose in its doom.

As in the case of "To his Heart . . . ," the use of images based on, or modelled upon, secret ritual occurs within a dramatic framework also taken from that ritual.

Perhaps the most useful of these frameworks for Yeats was that of the vision, sometimes presented as a mystical illumination, at other times as a dream. The machinery of vision was not, of course, the exclusive province of the magical orders; Yeats had heard the stories of peasant visionaries from earliest childhood and had himself attempted to cultivate the art of second sight during a long stay with the eccentric George Pollexfen.[23] It was, however, only after exposure to the organized visionary activities of Madame Blavatsky and crew that he gained the assurance and perspective to utilize the vision as a poetic device. Too, as has been noted earlier, his exposure to the actual process of conjuration and confrontation of the supernatural enhanced his intuitive grasp of what might be called the mechanics of exalted terror. An exemplary result is the starkly effective drop from visionary to human level in the opening lines of "The Unappeasable Host," spoken by a peasant mother:

> The Danaan children laugh in cradles of wrought gold,
> And clasp their hands together, and half close their eyes,
> For they will ride the North where the ger-eagle flies,
> With heavy whitening wings, and a heart fallen cold:
> I kiss my wailing child and press it to my breast,
> And hear the narrow graves calling my child and me.

Partly because of the old Irish peasant belief that the supernatural was directly contiguous to human life, and partly because of Yeats' conception of the spiritually animated universe, vision lurks everywhere in the landscapes of *The Countess Kathleen*, *The Celtic Twilight*, and *The Wind Among the Reeds*. The man attuned to spiritual voices is confronted by a message of his tragic destiny "Where wind cries in the sedge" or by a vision of the loved one in the curlew's cry. In "The Man who dreamed of Faeryland" Yeats moves with dexterous smoothness from the material world to the immaterial. In four parallel instances an image of worldly preoccupation and its corresponding reward is rendered trivial by the encroachment

[23] See the *Autobiographies*, pp. 154–162.

of a vision of a far higher order of happiness, the agents of vision being represented respectively by fish, a lug worm, a small "knot-grass," and worms.

Several of the poems in the collections mentioned above are introduced as dream visions—"I dreamed that one had died in a strange place"; "I dreamed that I stood in a valley." This device, one of the most conventional and innocuous means of passing into the visionary realm, is of little interest in the early Yeats with one exception—"The Valley of the Black Pig":

> The dew drips slowly and dreams gather: unknown spears
> Suddenly hurtle before my dream-awakened eyes,
> And then the clash of fallen horsemen and the cries
> Of unknown perishing armies beat about my ears.
> We who still labour by the cromlech on the shore,
> The grey cairn on the hill, when day sinks drowned in dew,
> Being weary of the world's empires, bow down to you,
> Master of the still stars and of the flaming door.

Here Yeats exhibits his mastery of the dramatic psychology of trance, bringing the seer toward his vision through the ominous twilight of present reality, and flinging him suddenly *in medias res*—but not among familiar things. The "spears" and the "perishing armies" are "unknown," thus portentous and terrifying; while the chaotic violence of apocalypse is driven home by such diction as "hurtle," "clash," "cries," and "beat." The focus upon "We" in line five is the signal for a shift from vision to the aftermath of vision, in which the seer must live with a new and awe-inspiring knowledge. In the last line both scene and seer are subordinated to a mysterious cosmic presence somehow responsible for the doomsday gesture. I disagree with Grossman when he says:

> The important thing about the poem is that the anticipated cataclysm does not take place. . . . In the end the impulse to throw off the burden of mortality is abandoned, the speaker sinks back into the paralysis of twilight, and the pre-existing order of things . . . is reasserted. (p. 96)

Surely the important thing is that the speaker, or seer, now *waits* for the apocalypse, which—far from failing to "take place" —is regarded as inevitable, according to a revelation from Anima Mundi. Also the notion of "labor" in line five is inconsistent with the "paralysis" which Grossman finds; rather, it suggests continuing active servitude to the "Master," as the phrase "Weary of the worlds' empires" implies eagerness for the end of those empires which the Master will bring about.

Apocalypse is a recurrent motif in *The Wind Among the Reeds*, and is obviously intended to support the general impression of tragedy's cosmic arena for which Yeats is striving. Nor only does the lover-initiate move and act among ultimates, but his private temporality somehow expands to touch upon the cataclysmic end of all time. There is an abundance of references to this end—"Til Time be no more"; "Time drops in decay"— most of them connected with the lover's desire for an end to the restlessness and flux which torment him. Such is obviously the case in "He mourns for the Change that has come upon him and his Beloved, and longs for the End of the World." The poem closes with an image unmistakably related to "The Valley of the Black Pig":

> I would that the Boar without bristles had come from
> the West
> And had rooted the sun and moon and stars out of the sky
> And lay in the darkness, grunting, and turning to his rest.[24]

At times, as in *King Lear*, the shaking of the world's foundations seems to form the milieu congenial to deeds of heroic moment; magnificent gestures, such as that of Cuchulain who "lost the world and Emer for a kiss," or that of "him who drove the gods out of their liss" will again become possible when the Rose drives all before it in apocalypse:

[24] Yeats explains in a footnote to the original text of "He mourns for..." in *The Dome* for June, 1897, that "... the boar without bristles is the ancient Celtic image of the darkness which will at last destroy the world, as it destroys the sun at nightfall in the west." See VE, p. 153.

> . . . I, too, await
> The hour of thy great wind of love and hate.
> When shall the stars be blown about the sky,
> Like the sparks blown out of a smithy, and die?
> Surely thine hour has come, the great wind blows,
> Far-off, most secret, and inviolate Rose?
>
> ("The Secret Rose")

Most of the visionary scenes in Yeats' poetry of the Nineties, whether presented as sudden illumination or dream, center upon the loved one, the woman whose "fatal" qualities function on a plane transcending the physical and mental wreckage to which Swinburne's hapless lovers are reduced. Indeed, her presence is a powerful catalyst to spiritual vision since, as noted above, her state of being is closely involved with some conception of ultimate reality. Like the Rose (with which at times she becomes synonymous), she encompasses the totality of tragic experience in the mysterious depths of her existence:

> When my arms wrap you around I press
> My heart upon the loveliness
> That has long faded from the world;
> The jeweled crowns that kings have hurled
> In shadowy pools, when armies fled;
> The love-tales wove with silken thread
> By dreaming ladies upon cloth
> That has made fat the murderous moth. . . .
>
> ("He remembers Forgotten Beauty")

Yeats intends here a notion of immanence more complex than the elevation by association which is the function of the conventional epic allusion, but such elevation is certainly a desired side effect. In this case the august company is that of noble beauty, sorrowfully fallen. Yeats later used a similar but more specific catalogue in revising "The Sorrow of Love":

> A girl arose that had red mournful lips
> And seemed the greatness of the world in tears,

> Doomed like Odysseus and the labouring ships
> And proud as Priam murdered with his peers.

When the woman's spirit is tormented, the unrest grows to cosmic proportions and conjures up the vision of crescendoing violence, of the gathering of malignant powers which can only be restrained by her return to the sad calm of tragedy's aftermath. She is thus allied, however unconsciously, with the ultimate controller of the universe, the "Master of the still stars and of the flaming door." It is from these considerations that Yeats' poem "He bids his Beloved be at Peace" acquires significance:

> I hear the Shadowy Horses, their long manes a-shake,
> Their hoofs heavy with tumult, their eyes glimmering white;
> . . . .
> O vanity of Sleep, Hope, Dream, endless Desire,
> The Horses of Disaster plunge in the heavy clay:
> Beloved, let your eyes half close, and your heart beat
> Over my heart, and your hair fall over my breast,
> Drowning love's lonely hour in deep twilight of rest,
> And hiding their tossing manes and their tumultuous feet.

Yeats dramatizes the spiritual portentousness of the "Beloved" by intensifying the significance of feminine gesture and attitude which he had learned from the Pre-Raphaelites. The graceful, stylized movement expands into a symbolic act of universal ramifications, demonstrating the theorem that the innermost processes of being are subordinated to the power of beauty in its Platonic dimension. Thus, the heroine of the poem above brings peace by falling into a languorous Pre-Raphaelite attitude; in "He gives his Beloved certain Rhymes," the significant gesture is the pinning of hair:

> You need but lift a pearl-pale hand,
> And bind up your long hair and sigh;
> And all men's hearts must burn and beat;
> And candle-like foam on the dim sand,

And stars climbing the dew-dropping sky,
Live but to light your passing feet.

The tragic power immanent in beauty, which not only outlines
heroes and dynasties, but is responsible for driving them to destruction, is symbolized by the "mournful" expression upon the
lips of Helen and Deirdre, who are represented as mortal embodiments of the Immortal Rose in "The Rose of the World":

Who dreamed that beauty passes like a dream?
For these red lips, with all their mournful pride,
Mournful that no new wonder may betide,
Troy passed away in one high funeral gleam,
And Usna's children died.

Though the "mournful" lips represent something eternal
and formidable they are not so themselves, and there is more
than a trace here of Yeats' fascination with gesture and attitude as slight, casual causes which bring forth profound tragic
effects. In the discrepancy lies an important element of the
heroic as Yeats conceived it: the enviable magnanimity of spirit
which made men court, and win, disaster for some single passing delight—which made Cuchulain, in a line quoted above,
lose . . . "the world and Emer for a kiss." This characteristic
must be taken into consideration among others as we turn from
a focus upon the qualities of the admired to a focus upon the
attitude of the admirer, the basic Yeatsian hero of the Nineties.

The elements of heroic renunciation and sacrifice on the one
hand, and of positive action in confrontation with the powers
of the air on the other, are present in the three relationships
with the tragic heroine which Yeats explores in *The Wind
Among the Reeds*. In a footnote to that collection he differ-
entiated between three personae:*

I have used them [Aedh, Hanrahan, and Michael Robartes]

* The personae now referred to in the titles as "He," "The Lover,"
or "The Poet" were originally called "Hanrahan," "Aedh," or "Michael
Robartes."

more as principles of the mind than as actual personages. It is probable that only students of the magical tradition will understand me when I say that 'Michael Robartes' is fire reflected in water and that Hanrahan is fire blown by the wind, and that Aedh, whose name is not merely the Irish form of Hugh, but the Irish for fire, is fire burning by itself. To put it in a different way, Hanrahan is the simplicity of an imagination too changeable to gather permanent possessions, or the adoration of the shepherds; and Michael Robartes is the pride of the imagination brooding upon the greatness of its possessions, or the adoration of the Magi; while Aedh is the myrrh and frankincense that the imagination offers continually before all that it loves. (VE, p. 803)

It might be argued, of course, that Yeats *hopes* only "students of the magical tradition" will understand his esoteric images, but it is possible for the non-initiated to trace in these images a logic which coalesces with the author's explanations of them. If the burning of the fire is regarded as the process of imaginative creation in its highest Coleridgean sense, then the reflection of this fire in water represents the detachment and perspective which are identified with the supreme initiate of the occult, Michael Robartes. Conscious of the long tradition which links beauty and the world of spirit, he exhibits a mode of homage to woman which depends upon erudition and historical awareness, and justifies Yeats' conception of it as "the adoration of the Magi." It is he who catalogues the "jewelled crowns" and "ancient love-tales" which inhere in beauty in the poem quoted above, and who gives the chronology of noble wonders connected with the "Hearts of wind-blown flame" and the "Winds older than changing of night and day":

> That murmuring and longing came
> From marble cities load with tabors of old
> In dove-gray faery lands;
> From battle-banners, fold upon perfect fold,
> Queens wrought with glimmering hands;
> That saw young Niamh hover with love-lorn face

> Above the wandering tide;
> And lingered in the hidden, desolate place
> Where the last Phoenix died. . . .
>
>> ("He [Michael Robartes] asks Forgiveness...")

The fact that this catalogue is part of an invocation which Robartes is teaching the "Beloved" to repeat points to his closely related role as the initiated conductor of those who are beginning on the path of the arcane, a role seen at its most extensive in the hyper-Paterian unravellings of the prose sketch "Rose Alchemica." Here Robartes, looking "something between a debauchee, a saint, and a peasant," appears to lead the aesthete-author into the intricacies of the "Order of the Alchemical Rose." [25] It appears again in the poetry in "He [Michael Robartes] bids his Beloved be at Peace," where he exhibits his familiarity with the ominous "Shadowy Horses" and attempts to advise and comfort the woman.

Far more human and fallible is Hanrahan, whose "fire blown by the wind" must be understood in terms of Yeats' wind symbol in *The Wind Among the Reeds*. A footnote to "He asks Forgiveness . . ." explains: "I use the wind as a symbol of vague desires and hopes, not merely because the Sidhe are in the wind, or because the wind bloweth as it listeth, but because wind and spirit and vague desire have been associated everywhere." [26] These desires, which torment the imagination of Hanrahan and frustrate its chance to partake of permanence and fulfillment as Robartes' partakes, are partly the result of a temperament naturally restless and capricious, partly the result of a curse placed upon the persona by Cleena of the Wave, whom he had scorned in a story in *The Secret Rose*: "Sorrow be upon him who rejects the love of the daughters of Dana, for he shall find no comfort in the love of the daughters of Eve." [27] The curse is seen in action in "He [Hanrahan] reproves

---

[25] *Mythologies* (London, 1959), p. 271.
[26] VE, p. 806.
[27] W. B. Yeats, *The Secret Rose* (London, 1897), pp. 154–155.

the Curlew," where the bird's cry brings the painful image of the beloved to the hero's mind, and in the story "The Twisting of the Rope and Hanrahan the Red" he is tricked outside the cabin and away from the side of a girl who has fallen in love with him. The scale of his torment is evident in the lyric which he sings as he enters the cabin:

> I never have seen Maid Quiet
> Nodding her russet hood,
> For the winds that awakened the stars
> Are blowing through my blood.
> I never have seen Maid Quiet
> Nodding alone and apart,
> For the words that called up the lightning
> Are calling through my heart.
>
> ("Maid Quiet")

Openly rebellious against the Catholic clergy, he represents a fierce and rowdy paganism which damns him in eternity by Christian standards as he has been damned on earth by Cleena's curse; thus the pathos of his plea to the Christian "colleens" is mixed with the tragic pagan image of a life consciously sacrificed to the service of the beloved in "The Lover [Hanrahan] speaks...":

> Bend down and pray for the great sin I wove in song,
> Till Maurya of the wounded heart cry a sweet cry,
> And call to my beloved and me: 'No longer fly
> Amid the hovering, piteous, penitential throng.'

Aedh, the last of the personae, appears as a bard of the royal court in *The Secret Rose*. At first he sings of war, but he himself becomes a victim of it; the story closes with his severed head singing the love lyric later entitled "Aedh gives his Beloved certain Rhymes." This poem, in which the machinations of the universe are made subservient to the woman's passing feet, illustrates that process of sublimation by which the power of the imagination passes directly into fantastic homage for the imagination's object; thus "fire burning by itself," not in the

remove of reflection or the distraction of wind. His is the
bardic function of celebration, and his sacrifice consists of re-
nouncing everything in life but the fashioning of "rhymes" in
the service of the beloved. Ritual self-abasement is one of his
common themes:

> Had I the heavens' embroidered cloths,
> Enwrought with golden and silver light,
> The blue and the dim and the dark cloths
> Of night and light and the half-light,
> I would spread the cloths under your feet:
> But I, being poor, have only my dreams;
> I have spread my dreams under your feet;
> Tread softly because you tread on my dreams.
>
> ("He [Aedh] wishes for the Cloths of Heaven")

Grossman, in an extended and revealing study of these three
personae, finds the distinction between their respective modes
of speech to be blurred:

> Since Yeats applied this systemization to the poetic speakers of
> *The Wind* in most cases after the composition and publication
> of the poems to which they are assigned, it is hardly remarkable
> that it is difficult to determine the appropriateness in each case
> of the speaker to the poem. (p. 107)

It seems to me that "in each case" goes rather far here. Admittedly the roles of the three personae occasionally overlap,
as when the hero of "He [Aedh] hears the cry of the Sedge"
suffers the tormenting separation from the beloved which usually characterizes Hanrahan; but they follow the categories discussed above consistently enough to preserve their antonomy.
And retrospective assignment of speakers does not imply that
Yeats was not conscious of variation in dramatic mode when
he first wrote the lyrics. It is true, nonetheless, that Yeats abol-
ished the distinction between them in the title of the poems
which appeared in the 1906 edition of his works, substituting
for all three names the neutral pronoun "He." Whatever his
reason—perhaps a wish to reaffirm the fact that three "prin-

ciples of mind" in the same lover rather than three separate lovers were being dramatized, perhaps a wish to escape "exotic" nomenclature—he had warrant for the amalgamation in the common mode of dramatic speech which the personae shared; and it is here that we come upon a facet of Yeats' development in the Nineties paralleled in significance only by his discoveries in symbolism.

Although the daemonic vein could furnish a great deal of animation and energy it was not—as Shelley's poems had shown—the sole requirement for dramatic power. Some attention was due to careful sentence structure and arrangement as well, and in *The Wind Among the Reeds* Yeats began to achieve a command of what he would later call "a powerful and passionate syntax." This syntax was revealed in effective combinations of dramatic address with imperative verbs suggesting starkly simple but significant actions; in the exploitations of certain potentialities inherent in the subjunctive mode and the future tense; and in a sense of pace which contained the whole in an effective pattern of rhetorical periods. Take, for example, "He thinks of those who have Spoken Evil of his Beloved":

> Half close your eyelids, loosen your hair,
> And dream about the great and their pride;
> They have spoken against you everywhere,
> But weigh this song with the great and their pride;
> I made it out of a mouthful of air,
> Their children's children shall say they have lied.

The opening compound imperative abruptly establishes a dramatic relationship, the more so in that its commands imbue the woman with a well-defined pose and even a mental attitude congruous with heroic pronouncement. In the third line Yeats leaves the imperative for the factual, but returns to command in the fourth; in the fifth he drops to reflection on the past, and rises to prophecy in the closing line, which is also the weightiest and most pointed. The use of variation here, interweaving the factual with the strongly dramatic, is decisive in giving this passage an aura of living dialogue, but is not the sum of Yeats' rhetorical skill. There still remain the antithetical balancing of lines three and five, the "mouthful of air" against the ubiquitous libel of "the great"; the sudden change of perspective in six as the future tense brings the force of posterity against the present, rendering it false and obsolete; and finally the neat rounding of the whole into a single balanced statement with rhetorical force. Conspicuous by its absence in the sort of superfluous visual description which plagued Yeats in the Arcadian days; all is stripped to the essence of forceful utterance, and the sense of urgent situation reigns supreme. One suspects here an early victory in what Yeats called his "war against the sedentary element in speech." [28]

That Yeats had attempted to give dramatic animation to his speech as extensively as he had sought to animate the cosmos becomes obvious in poems such as "To his Heart, bidding it have no Fear," and "He [Michael Robartes] asks Forgiveness because of his Many Moods." The opening imperative of the former—"Be you still, be you still, trembling heart"—is followed by the admonitory speech of an unidentified sage. The latter poem encloses within the dramatic address to the beloved—"If this importunate heart trouble your peace . . ."—an elaborate invocation which she is instructed to use and which is quoted, like the sages' speech, directly: "O Hearts of wind-blown flame! / O winds. . . . "

It is not at once evident, perhaps, that modes and tenses of verbs have inherent aesthetic characteristics, but some attempt was made in the analysis above to illustrate Yeats' exploitation of the future tense and its prophetic, judicial overtones. These may be found as well in "The Fish," where Yeats threateningly contrasts future and present through the prediction: "The people of coming days will know. . . ." More significant for his later development was his discovery of the uses of the subjunc-

[28] From a letter of Yeats quoted by Monk Gibbon in *The Masterpiece and the Man* (London, 1959), p. 137.

tive, which he would later employ in a hundred nuances from nostalgia to furious regret for lost opportunity, all of them suggesting the poignancy—in some cases the sense of tragic loss— which permeates a present under pressure from a hypothetical and unattainable realm of past possibilities. Such a pressure at times becomes part of the heroic burden, and the unanalyzable faint ring of the lofty archaic in the inversion "Had I . . ." reinforces the usefulness of the mode in the elevated but simple style of speech which Yeats was striving to construct. Although he would not begin to exploit the mode fully until *The Green Helmet*, there is more than a hint of later power in the extended subjunctive exercise "He wishes his Beloved were Dead," and in one of the most characteristic of this persona's verses, "He wishes for the Cloths of Heaven," which is quoted in full above.

It is true that Yeats does not always manage to sustain a sense of the powerful rhetorical period in his poetry of the Nineties; the syntax lapses into the repetitiousness of catalogue in parts of "He bids his Beloved be at Peace" and "He mourns for the Change. . . . " (See Chap. IV, p. 146.) Nonetheless, at its best his dramatic speech is unequalled by anything else in the verse of that period. When one looks past the mystical apparatus and esoteric symbolism, a degree of the tragic urgency and elevation which will distinguish the rhetorical constructions of the mature work are already evident and are instrumental, along with the sense of the daemonic, in distinguishing Yeats' poetry from that of his contemporaries and immediate predecessors. The distinction has not always been made, however, by the poet's critics, most of whom have remarked upon the *similarity* of Yeats's language to that of Rossetti and the Rhymers. Thomas Parkinson, for instance, asserts:

> The basic vocabulary of . . . ("The Two Trees")—exclusive of the occult symbols—is not in any important way distinct from that of other poets of the 'nineties, Lionel Johnson or Arthur Symons. Although the language is at a great remove from the

colloquial . . . the poem maintains a relation to actual speech: the syntax is free of inversions, and the poem strives to simulate the dramatic structure of address, in which the poet speaks to another person and is overheard by his audience in the process.[29]

One might say of Parkinson's statement that it is correct in general spirit, but needs strong qualifications both in particulars and in conclusion. Certainly Yeats shared with the other Rhymers a sort of "classical" concern for avoiding upholstered diction and contorted syntax, but paths of avoidance do not necessarily coincide. In the first place the vocabularies, outside "The Two Trees" at least, are not all that similar. Yeats' is filled with manifestations of such elementals as fire, wind, and water; with specifically Irish terms such as "cromlech," "cairn," "Danaan," and "host"; and with phrases from cabalistic lore in which the words acquire a significance beyond their normal denotations. Furthermore, the other Rhymers frequently utilize the archaic second person pronouns "thee" and "thine," and the corresponding verb forms, giving a sense of poetical diction to passages otherwise composed of current words.

The greatest linguistic difference, however, lies in Yeats' superior mastery of dramatic syntax and period, as reflected in the principles of rhetorical variation and the use of dramatic structures such as the imperative, discussed above. Dowson and Johnson are also fond of dramatic address, but they seldom attempt to sustain its animation and immediacy after the initial vocative; instead, they tend to lapse into a discursive syntax of contemplation, in which a series of qualifying phrases cast as factual remembrances or rhetorical questions interrupt the directness of the utterance. A stanza from Johnson's poem "The Destroyer of a Soul" will serve as an extreme example:

> I hate you with a necessary hate.
> First, I sought patience: passionate was she:

[29] *W.B. Yeats Self Critic* (Berkeley and Los Angeles, 1951), p. 16.

> My patience turned in very scorn of me,
> That I should dare forgive a sin so great,
> As this, through which I sit disconsolate;
> Mourning for that live soul, I used to see;
> Soul of a saint, whose friend I used to be:
> Till you came by! a cold corrupting fate.

At yet other times directness is mitigated by a predilection for neat quatrains musical rather than dramatic in intent, as in Dowson's "Exile":

> By the sad waters of separation
>   Where we have wandered by divers ways,
> I have but the shadow and imitation
>   Of the old memorial days.
> In music I have no consolation,
>   No roses are pale enough for me;
> The sound of the waters of separation
>   Surpasseth roses and melody.

It is not the rhetorical structure alone, of course, which gives the effect of rumination; the general tendency of Dowson and Johnson to describe emotional states rather than dramatize them is even more instrumental, and here we perhaps encounter once again the shadow of Tennyson.

These considerations are slightly ironic in light of the criterion which the Rhymers set themselves of testing a poem by its effectiveness when read aloud. Yeats discusses this standard in "The Tragic Generation":

> The meetings were always decorous and often dull; someone would read out a poem and we would comment, too politely for the criticism to have great value; and yet that we read our poems, and thought that they could be so tested, was a definition of our aims. *Love's Nocturne* is one of the most beautiful poems in the world, but no one can find out its beauty, so intricate its thought and metaphor, till he has read it over several times, or stopped several times to re-read a passage, and the *Faustine* of Swinburne, where much is powerful and musical, could not,

were it read out, be understood with pleasure, however clearly it were read, because it has no more logical structure than a bag of shot. I shall, however, remember all my life that evening when Lionel Johnson read or spoke aloud in his musical monotone, where meaning and cadence found the most precise elocution, his poem suggested 'by the Statue of King Charles at Charing Cross.' It was as though I listened to a great speech. . . . For long I knew only Dowson's 'O Mars' . . . and his 'Villanelle of Sunset' from his reading. . . . They were not speech but perfect song, though song for the speaking voice. (EI, pp. 180–181)

In complaining of the arbitrary "shot-bag" order of stanzas which prevailed in so many late nineteenth-century lyrics, Yeats puts his finger upon a primary obstacle to organic unity; but how could he exempt from transgression Johnson's poem "By the Statue of King Charles at Charing Cross"? Fine as it is, the poem has thirteen stanzas which unfold in an order far from inevitable; neither is there tight logic in Dowson's "Carthusians," or in his villanelles, which Yeats so admired. Certainly these poets achieved a general clarity of speech lacking in Rossetti's synaesthetic realms and Swinburne's purple haze, but their achievements in form do not suggest the tight logic of dramatic speech as do Yeats' verses "He thinks of those who have Spoken Evil" or "The Lover pleads with his Friend for Old Friends," both of which fall with the molded perfection of water drops. Yeats himself mitigates his defense somewhat by pointing out that Dowson's poems were "not speech but perfect song" and that the effectiveness of Johnson's poem was dependent upon his "musical monotone" rather than its intrinsic dramatic structure.

Yeats' early progress in arriving at a quality of passionate speech in the lyric demonstrates a divergence in technique from the Rhymers which fits in with the divergences in subject matter, scope, and energy noted earlier. Although there are enough languorous and twilit passages in Yeats' poetry of the Nineties to justify some use of the description "fin-de-siècle," it would be unfortunate if the term obscured the signs of dramatic animation, tragic elevation, and elemental concern which were already beginning to suggest the presence of a major poet in a decade of minor poetry. If a primary characteristic of literary "decadence" is the systematic exhaustion of once-vital strains and motifs, then the Neo-Romanticism of the Pre-Raphaelites and the lingering Victorianism of the Rhymers come closer to qualifying for that category than does the early work of Yeats, who developed—as we have seen—in a unique direction by channeling Shelleyan energy into his own dramatic modes and by involving himself with arcana which reinforced and freshened his heroic-daemonic bent. Closely linked with this bent, of course, was a growing tendency toward symbolic writing—one of the most individuating factors of all with respect to Yeats' English contemporaries, and an aspect of his early career which calls for detailed examination on its own.

IV

The Nascence of Yeats' Symbolism

IN TURNING TO A DISCUSSION OF YEATS' EARLY development as a symbolist, we turn inevitably to a consideration of his relation to the major French poets of the late nineteenth century. It is this relation which has furnished one of the main foci of critical contention in Yeatsian scholarship, a contention first kindled by Symons' dedication of *The Symbolist Movement in Literature* to Yeats himself and subsequently fueled by Edmund Wilson's inclusion of Yeats among the disciples of Baudelaire, Mallarmé, and other *symbolistes* in *Axel's Castle*. Hone and Hough acquiesced in this inclusion; Ellmann and W. Y. Tindall vigorously dissented, insisting that Yeats' symbolism derived from quite other sources, and was not even of the same nature as that of the French poets.[1] Although the argument descended at times to the level of squabbling about exactly how much French Yeats knew, it was more or less settled in favor of the anti-French faction. After all, as Ellmann points out, Yeats' earliest forays into symbolism ante-

[1] See respectively: J.M. Hone, *W.B. Yeats, 1865–1939* (New York, 1943), p. 111; Hough, p. xviii; Ellmann, *Masks*, p. 55; Tindall, "The Symbolism of W.B. Yeats," *Accent*, V (Summer, 1940), pp. 203–211.

date his acquaintance with Symons, who introduced him to the contemporary literature of the Continent.

Some refinement has taken place in the debate over the years, but it is possible to make even clearer the complexity of French symbolism on the one hand, and the variety of Yeats' symbolic practices on the other. Mallarmé's attempt to synthesize myths, for example, and Maeterlinck's war with physicality represent activities of the French school which frequently overshadow that elaboration of individual symbols which has given the school its name, and these activities present either influences or parallels worth examining in connection with similar undertakings on the part of Yeats. By the same token, Yeats' progress from the fledgling symbolic techniques of "Oisin" to the accomplished mastery of the "Byzantium" poems has relations and parallels as well as antitheses with French practice which should be made explicit as qualifications of the generally accurate belief that his practice has its true roots in Irish mythology and arcane tradition. In fact, the portion of that progress which falls within the scope of this study serves as a useful framework for examining the matrix of Yeats' symbolism.

Ellmann has cited "The Wanderings of Oisin" as the poem in which "for the first time Yeats used symbols with a sure hand," and there is no reason to quarrel with this assertion unless one should wish to question mildly the degree of Yeats' surety at this stage.[2] What needs to be established is the type of symbolism being attempted. The nature of most of the symbolic images and relations, and the nature of the interpretations advanced suggest the peculiarly Shelleyan blend of *Prometheus Unbound*. The basic vehicle, which is furnished by an ancient myth, is reshaped and expanded by use of the more abstract and mechanical devices of allegory. The blissful island retreat which Niamh and Oisin enter in Book I is—like most of Yeats' early paradises—the direct descendant of Shelley's "isle 'twixt

[2] *Masks*, p. 55.

Heaven, Air, Earth and Sea" in *Epipsychidion*; and, although an island is part of the original myth, Yeats' development of the landscape recalls the idealized, artificial settings so prominent historically in the allegorical repertory. More obviously from this same repertory are the daemonic opponent and his chained captive in Book II, since their elusive outlines and representational quality are characteristic of personification. Their ultimate prototypes are obviously the antagonist and protagonist of *Prometheus Unbound*, but more immediate prototypes may be found in Yeats' own poem "The Two Titans," published in 1886. Ellmann has elucidated the allegory of this poem quite convincingly: the bound youth is Ireland, the monstrous hag who has enthralled him is England.[3] The point here is that the explicitly allegorical quality of the earlier poem emphasized the presence of allegorical elements in the later and parallel book of "Oisin." This presence is also adumbrated by the element of abstraction in such names as "Isle of Joy" and "Isle of Victories," and by the somewhat mechanical trichotomy of life's aspects into love, war, and repose.

The impression of mechanical arrangement is mitigated, however, by the mythical portions of the poem's fabric, which suggest instead an organic and archetypal experience. Just as the story of the original bringer of fire and his championship of mankind furnishes a deep core in human experience for Shelley's allegorical complexities, so the Oisin myth—with its basic and ultimate theme of man caught between the pull of utopian possibilities and nostalgia for an imperfect but familiar mortal lot—furnishes a core of validity and universality at the heart of Yeats' sometimes fantastic convolutions. Individual portions of the poem—such as the passage near the close where Oisin falls from his horse into the mire of humanity in an attempt to aid humanity—expand naturally to an ethical dimension through their literal coherence and immediacy of experience, and perhaps (from the Yeatsian viewpoint) through the sympathetic

[3] *Masks*, pp. 48–49.

vibrations which the archetypal nature of the myth would en-
gender in man's inherited consciousness.

The possibility broached in this latter consideration depends
in turn upon the possible coalescence of the respective functions of myth and symbol in Yeats' early aesthetic philosophy.
Certainly the poet viewed symbols as possessing the power to
call up images and presences from such a consciousness, as he
asserts in listing the three famous doctrines from "Magic":

(1) That the borders of our mind are ever shifting and that
many minds can flow into one another, as it were, and
create or reveal a single mind, a single energy.
(2) That the borders of our memories are as shifting, and that
our memories are a part of one great memory, the memory
of Nature herself.
(3) That this great mind and great memory can be evoked by
symbols. (EI, p. 28)

In turn, his explanation of the "intellectual symbol" in "The
Symbolism of Poetry" is illustrated by examples of a mythologi-
cal nature:

. . . if I look at the moon herself and remember any of her
ancient names and meanings, I move among divine people, and
things that have shaken off our mortality, the tower of ivory,
the queen of waters, the shining stag among enchanted woods,
the white hare sitting upon the hilltop, the fool of Faery with his
shining cup full of dreams, and it may be 'make a friend of one
of these images of wonder,' and 'meet the Lord in the air.' (EI,
pp. 161–162)

It is not too much to suppose that the myth *in toto* partakes, so
far as Yeats is concerned, of the functioning of specific powerful symbols which may form a part of it, as the chase of the
"harmless deer" by the "hound with one red ear" forms a part
of the Oisin legend. Certainly the French symbolists included
both the myth and the symbol within the same ultimate category of artistic technique. André Beaunier makes a distinction
between "la fable" and allegory, continuing: "mais le poète

symboliste retrouve dans la Fable ancienne l'eternel mystère incarné"; [4] and Mallarmé expends his major artistic energies in the mythopoeticizing of "Herodiade" and "L'Apres-Midi d'un Faun." That Yeats' theories of symbolism were developed to any extent at the time of "Oisin" is doubtful; he was, as has been indicated, following a Shelleyan conception by instinct, hoping to create "some new *Prometheus Unbound*" out of "Patrick or Columbkil, Oisin or Fion" (A, p. 119). It happened, however, that myth was an important part of that Shelleyan conception, and thus the groundwork was laid in "Oisin" for that intensely symbolical treatment of mythology, "The Shadowy Waters," with which Yeats would close the century.

Even in "Oisin," however, there was yet a second sort of symbolism, nascent but recognizable, which was closer to the sense in which the term is usually understood, and which would be of more significance for Yeats' mature art. It centered upon the use of specific creatures or objects which transcended their literal definitions and normal functions because of their portentous significations in the imaginative realm (or in Yeats' case the *Anima Mundi*) rather than upon the general expansion of myth or allegory to higher levels. The most obvious of the symbols in "Oisin" is the chase of the "hornless deer" by "a phanton hound / All pearly white, save one red ear." The image recurs again in "He mourns for the Change . . . " and yet again in "The Shadowy Waters." Yeats explains it in a footnote to the former:

> I got my hound and deer out of a last-century Gaelic poem about Oisin's journey to the country of the young. . . . This hound and this deer seem plain images of the desire of the man 'which is for the woman,' and the desire of the woman 'which is for the desire of the man,' and of all desires such as these. I have read them in this way in "The Wanderings of Oisin," and have made my lover sigh because he has seen in their faces 'the immortal desire of immortals.' (VE, p. 807)

[4] Quoted by A.G. Lehmann, *The Symbolist Aesthetic in France, 1885–1895* (Oxford, 1950), p. 253.

Yeats also recalls analogues in Arthurian and Welsh mythology, thus emphasizing the recurrence of the true symbol in "the Great Memory." It is unlikely, however, that this theory of 1899 was quite so explicit over ten years earlier during the composition of "Oisin." Taken over from Comyn's unsymbolic translation, the deer and hound do not quite emerge distinctly from the rest of the phantasmagoria of Oisin's adventures. They lack the ontological autonomy which gives the symbol much of its portentousness, and which Yeats would begin to infuse into his symbols later in the Nineties.

To this same category of specific symbols belong the objects which start Oisin into troubled reverie at the end of each episode, causing him to seek change. In Book I, it is "the staff of wood" from "some dead warrior's lance" which causes the hero to remember the exhilaration of his martial feats among the Fenians; the martial episode is in turn brought to an end by the sight of a "beech bough" which is bound up in Oisin's mind with an earlier time of twilight leisure in the company of friends when he watched the race of hares "Leap in the meadow"; and the final adventure on the Island of Sleep is terminated by the fall of "A starling" which suggests to him the wakefulness of early morning hunts with the Fenians, rather than repose. What is interesting is that Yeats discusses the peculiar memories stirred by each object in Oisin's mind, thus indicating in rough form a powerful process of association more or less analogous to that which functions on a grander scale when "intellectual symbols" act on an individual's portion of the Great Memory. Also, in both cases, the results of the process are something more than the mere aesthetic delight of perceived metaphors; Oisin is led to positive action, and the sensitive reader would be led, in Yeats' view of a few years later, to something approaching a visionary state.

The year 1889, which saw the use of Shelleyan myth-allegory and of Irish symbols in "Oisin," saw also the beginning of Yeats' collaboration with Edwin Ellis on an edition of Blake's poetry, with the resultant emergence of Blake as an important influence upon Yeats. This new influence did not, in fact, negate the old; Yeats was able to look back in one of his last essays and point out that it was Shelley who:

> ... had shared our curiosities, our political problems, our conviction that, despite all experience to the contrary, love is enough; and unlike Blake, isolated by an arbitrary symbolism, he seemed to sum up all that was metaphysical in English poetry. When in middle life I looked back I found that he and not Blake, whom I had studied with more and more approval, has shaped my life. . . . (EI, p. 424)

Nonetheless, Yeats as a young man assimilated much from Blake which would come to fruition in such later works as *A Vision*; and during this very period of assimilation there is an obvious "Blakean" phase in his poetry, which must qualify Bloom's basically correct assertion that the diction and syntax of Blake had little influence on the early Yeats. This phase is characterized by the entrance of "Heaven," "Hell," and "God" into Yeats' symbology, by the use of the brief and short-lined aphoristic stanza, and by embodiment of the symbolical import in a short fable. Blake's poem "The Clod and the Pebble" is perhaps characteristic of this mode:

> 'Love seeketh not Itself to please,
> Nor for itself hath any care,
> But for another gives its ease,
> And builds a Heaven in Hell's despair.'
> So sung a little Clod of Clay
> Trodden with the cattle's feet,
> But a Pebble of the brook
> Warbled out these metres meet:

> 'Love seeketh only Self to please,
> To bind another to Its delight,
> Joys in another's loss of ease,
> And builds a Hell in Heaven's despite.' [5]

[5] Blake, *Selected Poetry and Prose* (New York, 1953).

Compare with this Yeats' poem "The Rose of Peace," first published in 1892 when the collaborators were deep in Blake:

> If Michael, leader of God's host
> When Heaven and Hell are met,
> Looked down on you from Heaven's door-post
> He would his deeds forget.
>
> Brooding no more upon God's wars
> In his divine homestead,
> He would go weave out of the stars
> A chaplet for your head.
>
> And all folk seeing him bow down,
> And white stars tell your praise,
> Would come at last to God's great town,
> Led on by gentle ways;
>
> And God would bid His warfare cease,
> Saying all things were well;
> And softly make a rosy peace,
> A peace of Heaven with Hell.

The phrase "When Heaven and Hell are met" is particularly suggestive of Blake, not only in its combination of the enigmatic, epigrammatic, and prophetic, but in the parallel with the earlier poet's prose work "The Marriage of Heaven and Hell." There the eventual resolution of moral contrarieties brings an end to cosmic conflict such as Yeats envisages in his closing stanza: "And God would bid his warfare cease. . . . " The very notion of the warring Jehovah probably derives from Blake's militant form of mysticism, and Yeats' preoccupation in *The Wind Among the Reeds* with apocalypse and its peaceful aftermath may owe something to similar Blakean conceptions. These considerations are supported by the fact that similar phraseology and import may be found in a companion poem "The Rose of Battle," also published in 1892:

For God has bid them share an equal fate;
And when at last, defeated in His wars,
They have gone down under the same white stars,
We shall no longer hear the little cry
Of our sad hearts, that may not live nor die.

This period of the Blakean symbolic fable overlaps with the end of the "Irish fable" period which had included such productions as "Father Gilligan," "The Ballad of Father O'Hart," and "The Ballad of Moll Magee"; and the two simplistic modes involved are not always easily separable. There is an important difference, however, since the simplicity of the symbolic poetry is a rhetorical attempt to imitate the starkness of mystic utterance, whereas that of the Irish represents an attempt to reproduce the naïveté of the ballad. It is with the former sort of simplicity that we are dealing in a consideration of "The Cap and Bells," as the note which Yeats appended to the poem suggests:

> I dreamed this story exactly as I have written it, and dreamed another long dream after it, trying to make out its meaning, and whether I was to write it in prose or verse. The first dream was more a vision than a dream, for it was beautiful and coherent, and gave me the sense of illumination and exaltation that one gets from visions, while the second dream was confused and meaningless. The poem has always meant a great deal to me, though, as is the way with symbolic poems, it has not always meant quite the same thing. Blake would have said, 'The authors are in eternity,' and I am quite sure they can only be questioned in dreams. (VE, p. 808)

The enigmatic dream fable also has its specialized prototype in Blake, as witness "The Angel" in *Songs of Experience*, while the symbolic choice of Yeats' heroine is prefigured in Blake's choice of the "Rose-tree" over "such a flower as May never bore" in the pointed quatrains of "My Pretty Rose-Tree." The purport of the symbolism seems to be that the queen is oblivious both to her lover's offer of his entire emotional being—represented by the heart dressed in the red of corporeality—and to his offer of his entire spiritual being, represented by the soul dressed in a blue garment, anticipating Wallace Stevens' color symbol for the imagination; but she finally accepts both these highly serious aspects of the lover after being charmed by the "cap and bells" representative of his foolish, light-hearted side. Such an interpretation would be in keeping with Yeats' later concept of the "crazy salad" which charmed Helen and Aphrodite, and with the idea expressed in "Vacillation": "All women dote upon an idle man."

The symbol of the cap and bells, however, eventually leads us away from Blake to a study of French symbols which it resembles in its proximity to a truncated figure of speech. To consider the *"cap and bells* of a fool" is to consider a rhetorical concept not unlike the *"laurels* of a poet" or the *"mantle* of a leader"; in all cases, a concrete object closely associated with some active agent acquires an element of abstraction in its assimilation of the functions and attributes of that agent. When the agent's name is removed and the object is left in a figurative context, the object retains something of the ontological richness of its physicality, as well as a new element of freedom in its abstract components. John Crowe Ransom's contention that the "sea of troubles" in *Hamlet* contains not only the metaphorical waves to which Mr. Richards would limit it, but "fish" and "screaming birds" [6] as well, would be beyond dispute after the elliptical omission of the "troubles" and the placing of the "sea" in a symbolic context, where Mr. Ransom would have wildlife enow.

Thus, in Rimbaud's poem "Honte," it is the "blade of shame" which furnishes the central image, but it is not called this. It is simply "la lame," and is defined by its possible function of piercing the miscreant's brain—"Ce paquet blanc, vert et gras / A vapeur jamais nouvelle." [7] Similarly, Mallarmé's "Les Fenêtres" are "windows of the imagination" but the poet gains the

[6] Ransom, *The New Criticism*, p. 10.
[7] Rimbaud, *Oeuvres Complètes* (Paris, 1963).

portentousness of symbol for his organizing image by a careful synthesis of context rather than the appending of a trite phrase:

> Je fuis et je m'accroche à toutes les croisées
> D'où l'on tourne l'épaule à la vie, et, béni,
> Dans leur verre, lave, lavé d'éternelles rosées,
> Que dore le matin chaste de l'Infini.[8]

In "L'Azur," by the same poet, the basic figure is something like "the sky of infinite possibilities," but again we have dramatization of the symbol's expansion into significance in place of an explicitly limiting signpost.

One of the more striking technical similarities between Yeats' use of symbols and that of the *symbolistes* is found in an isolated occurrence in a poem published in 1890, "The Dedication to a Book of Stories selected from the Irish Novelists." The central image here, a "bell-branch," has not the common currency of windows and caps and bells, but acquires the same figurative character as the poem unfolds. What is most interesting, however, is the opening explanation of the symbol's background, an explanation which serves not only as an elucidation of meaning but as a preparation of the symbol's figurative context. Yeats begins by describing a magical and legendary bell-branch which brought spiritual ease to ancient Ireland, then makes a sudden change from the literal to the figurative with the line "I also bear a bell-branch full of ease," where the bell-branch becomes a symbol for the Irish stories which exercise, supposedly, an analogous effect. By differentiating between a concrete original and his own version of the branch, he makes clear the partially abstract nature of the latter, after having established a sense of physical reality which serves to drive the image home on the sensual level.

This symbolic technique, which verges at times on the overly explicit, is not usually associated with the French symbolists; but examination of their poems, particularly those of Baude-

[8] Mallarmé, *Poésies* (Paris, 1929).

laire and Mallarmé, shows its frequency. Consider, for instance, the former's "La Cloche fêlée." The opening stanzas describe and praise the literal bell which rings out roundly and clearly while the auditor sits listening "près du feu qui palpite et qui fume. . . . " In stanza three the figurative significance is immediately and obviously reached with the line "Moi, mon âmé est fêlée."; the persona's soul is seen to be an enfeebled maker of music, a cracked bell, which sounds more like "le râle épais d'un blessé." [9] Another and more famous poem by Baudelaire, "Le Cygne," exhibits the same movement, though in slightly more complex form. Here the primary symbol is a swan who has escaped his cage and drags his beautiful plumage through the filthy, waterless streets in dejection, "le coeur plein de son beau lac natal." Baudelaire says that he thinks of his "grand cygne, avec ses gestes fous . . . " and then "à vous, / Andromaque," thus specifying an obviously human element in the symbolic equation. He subsequently moves from antique particularity to timeless generality with the line "A quiconque a perdue ce qui ne se retrouve," and the levels of the symbol are explicitly marked out. Surely one of the most detailed preparations for the figurative sense is found in Mallarmé's "Les Fenêtres," the crucial transitional stanza of which was quoted above. Actually, this stanza is preceded by five others which describe almost microscopically the joyful window-gazing of an aged hospital patient who is thus able to stare at beautiful vistas which blot out the horror of his clinical surroundings. Pivoting upon the conjunction "Ainsi," the poet enlarges the hospital to the earth itself, with its ubiquitous spiritual squalor, and the windows—as indicated above—become windows of the soul.

It is no doubt this method of building the symbol which leads Edward Engelberg to conclude that "*symbolisme* moved toward a coalescing symbol [whereas] Yeats moved away from

---

[9] Baudelaire, *Oeuvres Complètes* (Paris, 1961). All subsequent citations of Baudelaire are to this edition.

an exfoliating one." [10] Certainly Engelberg's statement contains an important core of truth, but it contains also the doubtful assumption that coalescence was an end in itself for the *symbolistes* and the doubtful implication that the character of Yeats' symbols is more or less homogeneous. Actually, rather than desiring "effects that terminate in the symbol," Baudelaire and Mallarmé are quite concerned with the ultimate exfoliation of the symbol, and their labors are devoted to an exposition of the *correspondances* which illuminate experience, and are *inherent* in the symbol—although the later Yeats would insure this exfoliation by choosing more specific and historically defined symbols in the first place. As for Yeats' homogeneity, our considerations have indicated that his brand of symbolism varied with the passing of the years, and the remainder of this chapter will still further emphasize the diversity of that symbolism. All this is not by way of attempting to undermine Engelberg's conclusion, which the author admits is provisional, but is rather an attempt to stress the refining process through which any comparison of Yeats and the *symbolistes* must be carried.

It is unlikely that the parallelism in symbolic techniques between Yeats and the French is really anything more than accidental parallelism. The examples quoted from the former are, after all, isolated and not really representative; and the techniques themselves, involving as they do the formation symbols which border upon metaphor in the separability of Ransom's "vehicle and tenor," are the sort on which questing poets could easily stumble without outside influence. What is significant, perhaps, is the implication that Yeats *was questing*, and that symbolism was as yet to him a fluid, experimental mode. At any rate, early in the Nineties he began to experiment with a type of symbol far removed both from Shelleyan myth-allegory and from the type identified with the French. This was the arcane symbol, taken from cabalistic, theosophic, Rosicrucian, or

[10] Engelberg, *The Vast Design* (Toronto, 1964), p. 112.

druidic lore, and partly dependent upon its invocatory powers for its effectiveness.

This symbol finds its earliest ancestors in the beech boughs and hornless deer of "Oisin"; and with the bell-branch of the "Dedication," discussed above, the magical overtones enter explicitly. In this case, however, the purely figurative sense which Yeats develops obscures the arcane element, since the ancient Irish branch is merely used as a physical example to enhance the connotations of its abstract descendant. The first full-fledged example of the arcane symbol in Yeats' poetry is the Rose, which usurps the stage in imagery during the first half of the Nineties. The history of this symbol, which reaches back to Biblical times, has been traced by Barbara Seward in her study *The Symbolic Rose*. What concerns us is the nature of its reality in Yeats' verse, a subject on which the poet himself made several explicit statements. In a note to several poems in *The Wind Among the Reeds* he says: "The Rose has been for many centuries a symbol of spiritual love and supreme beauty" (VE, p. 211). Years later he makes casual but enlightening mention of the symbol's meaning in *The Rose*:

> . . . I notice upon reading these poems for the first time for several years that the quality symbolized by the Rose differs from the Intellectual Beauty of Shelley and Spenser in that I have imagined it as suffering with man and not as something pursued and seen from afar. (VE, p. 842)

The fusion of beauty and love into a unity at the top of their respective Neoplatonic hierarchies is a vague and complex phenomenon which gives to the Rose a tremendous symbolic burden; when the phenomenon is endowed with autonomous moment such as is suggested by Shelley's "awful shadow of some unseen Power" which "floats though unseen among us"; and when autonomous consciousness is added by the capability of "suffering with man," the total purport of the symbol is rendered well-nigh imponderable, as perhaps it is intended to be. At any rate, we are dealing not simply with the communication of a semantic complex by a single sign, but the *name* of some spirit or presence which is actually being invoked by such formulaic phrasings as "Far-off, most secret, and inviolate Rose."

This last distinction is of considerable importance to an understanding of the changing nature of Yeats' symbolism in the Nineties for it marks a turn away from emphasis upon the symbol's communicative function as a sort of shorthand for which there is no precise longhand equivalent, to a quite different function defined by the influence of the symbolic words upon mysterious forces independent of the human mind which are consequently brought to bear upon that mind. J.I.M. Stewart, perhaps the first to emphasize this distinction, finds in Yeats "an element of confusion between the symbols of magic and the symbols of poetry," [11] but Yeats' own statement attempts to reconcile the two varieties:

> All sounds, all colours, all forms, either because of their preordained energies or because of long association, evoke indefinable and yet precise emotions, or, as I prefer to think, call down among us certain disembodied powers, whose footsteps over our hearts we call emotions; and when sound and colour, and form are in a musical relation, a beautiful relation to one another they become, as it were, one sound, one colour, one form, and evoke an emotion that is made out of their distinct evocations and yet is one emotion.[12]

Here the influence of the "powers" is seen as a specifically aesthetic one, the evoking of emotional response, and they themselves are seen as intermediaries between word and reader. In fact, with the phrase "as I prefer," Yeats provides a trapdoor

[11] Stewart, *Eight Modern Writers* (Oxford, 1963), p. 313.

[12] EI, pp. 156–157. This statement of Yeats' theory, like Baudelaire's theory of *correspondances*, presents an initial difficulty in that it does not seem, on the surface, to distinguish between "all sounds" etc. and those portentous, particular things which are usually considered "symbols"; it seems likely, however, that some such distinction is inherent here in the mention of the "mystical relations" of sound, color, and form—a relation of particular power which evokes a more complex variety of emotion.

in the theory through which the unbeliever can eject the powers while retaining the gist of the statement on symbolic function.

The poems themselves give evidence of the close relation of the powers, particularly the Rose, to the poetic process. "To the Rose upon the Rood of Time" is a prayer for poetic inspiration, possible only when the Rose, by its proximity, clears away the bric-a-brac of mortality and opens the poet's eyes to "Eternal beauty wandering on her way." The poet pleads, however, that the Rose not come too near, causing him to lose touch completely with humanity. In "The Secret Rose" the symbol makes possible the artist's unity with the great heroes of the imagination, including:

> ... the king whose eyes
> Saw the Pierced Hands and Rood of elder rise
> In Druid vapour and make the torches dim.

This latter poem also exhibits the similarity of Yeats' concept of the function of the powers to the three tenets of symbolism quoted above from "Magic." If Cuchulain, the king, and the other heroes are somehow contained among "the great leaves" of the Rose, and thus made accessible to the poet, then their accessibility through symbolic provocation of the *Anima Mundi*, which also "enfolds" them, is analogous and perhaps synonymous. From either aspect, the proper manipulation of the symbol mysteriously produced "vision," which Yeats is never at great pains to separate into "poetic" and "mystic." The two blend together, especially in the poetry of the Nineties, which usually has for its subject matter some sort of supernatural vision. At this stage of Yeats' aesthetic it was not thought necessary to evolve a symbol carefully as a construct of intrinsic meaning, but merely to intone the name of a magical symbol, an arcane word or phrase which unlocked the storehouse of the Great Memory and produced the poetic-mystic condition of second sight. For Yeats, the "unknown perishing armies" which rise before his eyes in "The Valley of the Black Pig" are ontologically indistinguishable from the "visions" which he and George Pollexfen stimulated with symbolic designs painted on cards during the fantastic interludes at Sligo in the late Eighties.

Yeats' embracing of this brand of arcane symbolism raised some interesting problems in poetic technique and influenced his general style significantly during the Nineties. The complex Platonic character of the Rose, for example, as described above, was not easily susceptible of treatment in physical terms. The close association of the Rose with feminine beauty and its character as a living spirit cause the poet to describe it at times in terms of a woman, while at yet other times he feels the need to fill out the literal botanical aspects of the symbol by references to leaves and blossoms. Ellmann has noted that Yeats follows a pattern in his presentation of this symbol:

> Yeats either begins, then, with a symbolic abstraction and humanizes it, or begins with a woman and renders her symbolically impersonal. When she appears initially as a woman, she will, as like as not, begin shortly to unfold as a multifoliate rose to be sought unavailingly among mortal women. On the other hand, when she is a rose at the beginning of a poem, she generally ends up with characteristics that have nothing to do with the flower. (*Identity*, p. 74)

At whichever end he began, Yeats was faced with conceptual difficulties in respect to the sensual aspects of the symbol which were not presented by Mallarmé's movement from a literal window to a figurative one. The Rose, like the "axle . . . That keeps the stars in their round," and the "banners of East and West," [13] is a spiritual entity to which a familiar name has been given rather than a simple metaphorical vehicle from the concrete world, and it is this ontological complexity which underlies much of the wavering and vagueness of Yeats' arcane imagery.

The use of symbols frequently enhances the incantatory tone so common in Yeats' poems during this period. The mysterious status of the symbols, which hover somewhere between spirit

[13] "He hears the Cry of the Sedge."

and matter, interacts with the formulaic constructions and prophetic utterances in which the symbols are embedded to fashion a mode of speech suited to the frontier of the supernatural. Thus, "The starry winds and the flame and the flood" add a decisive element of the ominous to the Rosicrucian admonition which is their context in "To his Heart, bidding it have no Fear." Apocalyptic prophecies furnish a natural context for such symbols, since the potential revelation of the elemental symbol's nature is somehow bound up with the revelation of time's ultimate demise:

> Until the axle break
> That keeps the stars in their round,
> And hands hurl in the deep
> The banners of East and West,
> And the girdle of light is unbound,
> Your breast will not lie by the breast
> Of your beloved in sleep.

At times it is the symbol which seems specifically to call forth the ritualistic phrasings; this is particularly the case with the addressable Rose, which must be invoked as a spirit: "Red Rose, proud Rose, sad Rose of all my days!"; "Rose of all Roses, Rose of the world"; and, of course, "Far-off, most secret, and inviolate Rose."

As early as *The Wind Among the Reeds* Yeats was already struggling for a "passionate syntax" which would give his lyrics dramatic force. Occasionally, however, he relaxed that struggle and fell into the flat, sometimes repetitious structure of catalogue. Since it was usually symbols which were being catalogued, we may look at Yeats' theories of symbolism for some explanation of this lapse. The answer probably lies in the enormous catalytic powers attributed by Yeats to the symbol—powers which not only stimulated the reader's participation in the Great Memory, but supposedly invoked aesthetic spirits. It is not surprising that the symbol should come at times to seem self-sufficient and capable of giving rise to the experience of poetic vision without the benefit of careful dramatic context. Such an observation provides a plausible reason for the sheer density of symbolic images in "He thinks of his Past Greatness...":

> I have drunk ale from the Country of the Young
> And weep because I know all things now:
> I have been a hazel-tree, and they hung
> The Pilot Star and the Crooked Plough
> Among my leaves in times out of mind. . . .

and in "The Poet pleads with the Elemental Powers":

> The Powers whose name and shape no living creature knows
> Have pulled the Immortal Rose;
> And though the Seven Lights bowed in their dance and wept,
> The Polar Dragon slept. . . .

A certain syntactical monotony is evident in the catalogue of symbolic directions from "He bids his Beloved be at Peace." The parallelism may have some incantatory effect, but there is no doubt that it becomes slightly oppressive:

> The North unfolds above them clinging creeping night,
> The East her hidden joy before the morning break,
> The West weeps in pale dew and sighs passing away,
> The South is pouring down roses of crimson fire. . . .

This study of the arcane symbol and its usage in Yeats' poetry makes clear, among other things, the divergence of Yeats' basic symbolic techniques from those of his French predecessors and contemporaries; what remains to be ascertained is what he does owe to these poets. On this score, Yeats' own testimony is valuable but vague. He speaks in "The Tragic Generation" of the accomplished metrical translations which Symons made from Mallarmé, Verlaine, Calderon, and St. John of the Cross, and continues:

> . . . I think that those from Mallarmé may have given elaborate

form to my verses of those years, to the later poems of *The Wind Among the Reeds*, to *The Shadowy Waters*, while Villiers de L'Isle Adam had shaped whatever in my *Rosa Alchemica* Pater had not shaped. I can remember the day in Fountain Court when he [Symons] first read me Herodiade's address to some Sibyl who is her nurse and it may be the moon also:

> The horror of my virginity
> Delights me, and I would envelope me
> In the terror of my tresses, that, by night
> Inviolate reptile, I might feel the white
> And glimmering radiance of thy frozen fire,
> Thou that are chaste and diest of desire,
> White night of ice and of the cruel snow!
> Eternal sister, my lone sister, lo
> My dreams uplifted before thee! now, apart,
> So rare a crystal is my dreaming heart,
> And all about me lives but in mine own
> Image, the idolatrous mirror of my pride,
> Mirroring this Herodiade diamond-eyed.

Yet I am certain that there was something in myself compelling me to attempt creation of an art as separate from everything heterogeneous and casual, from all character and circumstance, as some Herodiade of our theatre, dancing seemingly alone in her narrow moving luminous circle. (A, p. 193)

The distinction which Yeats is interested in making in the last sentence is not between the art of Mallarmé and his own art, but between Mallarmé's influence and his own similar but natural instincts. The point is important because it must be seen that this last sentence is really a description of Mallarmé's art and thus an indication of the meaning of the mysterious phrase "elaborate form" which Yeats uses to characterize his debt. What he feels he shares with Mallarmé is a concern for form on that tragic level which transcends the sharp physicality of individual, or comic form, finding such realizable organization as it possesses in the temporary crystallization of daemonic elementals, such as the "glimmering radiance of . . . frozen fire" and "white night of ice" toward which Herodiade is drawn from a state already so characterless that it is defined only by the multiple mirrored images of the heroine.

It was not a new concern for Yeats, of course; we have seen its genesis in the statues and looming figures of the earliest poetry. In the work of Mallarmé and others, however, he found encouragement and impetus for certain artistic impulses which undoubtedly were, as he claims, inherent in his nature. One of the more important sources of encouragement was the work of the Belgian playwright Maeterlinck, whose name recurs again and again in Yeats' prose of the Nineties. Although Yeats had reservations almost from the start about Maeterlinck's ultimate stature—he told Verlaine in 1894 that the playwright sometimes touched "the nerves" rather than "the heart"—he recorded his enthusiasm for *Les Aveugles* and admitted that Maeterlinck was "of immense value as a force, helping people to understand a more ideal drama" (L, p. 255). Along with Villiers de l'Isle-Adam, whose *Axël* was one of Yeats' "sacred books" during this period, Maeterlinck is given credit for spearheading the movement toward an essential etherealized drama which Yeats saw at the time as the direction of artistic salvation:

> . . . Count Villiers de l'Isle-Adam . . . created persons from whom has fallen all even of personal characteristic except a thirst for that hour when all things shall pass away like a cloud, and a pride like that of the Magi following their star over many mountains; while Maeterlinck has plucked away even this thirst and this pride and set before us faint souls, naked and pathetic shadows already half vapour and sighing to one another upon the border of the last abyss. (EI, p. 190)

Characterization in Maeterlinck does indeed seem the vague outlining of "faint souls" who face the "last abyss" bereft of normal human resources; in *Les Aveugles* the cast consists of thirteen blind people, a dead priest, an infant, and a dog. The differentiation of the blind, aside from sex, is limited to age, degrees of blindness (some were born blind; one can distinguish light and darkness) and, in isolated cases, insanity and deafness. None is called by name, and most of the dialogue consists of the exchange of single sentences, a technique which increases the ethereal nature of the proceedings, especially when combined with the pervading insubstantiality of the world of the blind, and with synaesthesia:

Premier Aveugle-Né

La voix résonne comme si nous étions dans une grotte.

Le Plus Vieil Aveugle

Je crois plutôt qu'elle résonne ainsi parce que c'est le soir.

La Jeune Aveugle

Il me semble que je sens le clair de lune sur mes mains.

La Plus Vieille Aveugle

Je crois qui'il y a des étoiles; je les entends.

La Jeune Aveugle

Moi aussi.

Premier Aveugle-Né

Je n'entends aucun bruit.

Deuxième Aveugle-Né

Je n'entends que le bruit de nos souffles!

Le Plus Vieil Aveugle

Je crois que les femmes ont raison.

Premier Aveugle-Né

Je n'ai jamais entendu les étoiles.[14]

The abyss becomes evident when the blind people discover that the priest who guided them into the wood is dead, and that they are hopelessly lost. Stark terror prevails as mysterious steps approach and the infant, who can see, begins to weep desperately at something which stops in the midst of the group. This ending is similar to that of another Maeterlinck play, *L'Intruse*, where the blind grandfather senses that some mysterious being has risen from the table, and moments later the death of his daughter is announced.

[14] Maeterlinck, *L'Intruse et Les Aveugles*, ed. H.W. Church (New York, 1925).

Yeats' own *dramatis personae* in the later poems of *The Wind Among the Reeds* exhibit a corresponding tendency toward disembodiment, and the image of the world as a habitat dissolving into a vague and fiery flux becomes increasingly frequent. No longer do we find the solidity of "The heavy steps of the ploughman, splashing the wintry mould"—a line from a poem written in 1892 under the last vestiges of Irish-ballad influence;[15] instead, the poems after 1895 are peopled with "the Shadowy Horses"; "the unappeasable host"; "the unlabouring brood of the skies"; women with "cloud-pale eyelids" and "pearl-pale hands"; and with Irishmen seen not as flesh and blood but as walking "souls" in a vision of "drifting smoke." In addition, the various images of apocalypse, such as the stars "blown about the sky," along with such furnishings as "the flaming lute-thronged angelic door," help to define an environment where normal physicality has given way to some realm of Platonic essences. This intangibility, implying a progress away from the bonds of the material, is reflected also in the world of Yeats' long dramatic poem "The Shadowy Waters," begun in the Eighties but not finished until 1900. What the "Other Sailor" has been walking on the water is "something bearded like a goat," an image characterized by the Maeterlinckean terror of the indefinite, and Forgael's destination is described in the dream vision:

> . . . of an hour
> When earth and heaven have been folded up;
> And languors that awake in mingling hands
> And mingling hair fall from the fiery boughs
> To lead us to the streams where the world ends.[16]
>
> (ll. 365–369)

These tendencies toward etherealization were present in Yeats'

---

[15] "The Lover tells of the Rose in his Heart."

[16] Printed in *The North American Review*, May 1900, and reprinted in VE, pp. 746–769. All subsequent citations of "The Shadowy Waters" are to this version.

poetry, of course, long before he came to Mallarmé and Maeterlinck; this much is obvious from his early immersion in Shelley and his natural bent toward treatment of the supernatural. It seems likely, however, that the tendencies were greatly reinforced by a belief encouraged by these French contemporaries that the mainstream of poetry had turned in a direction more or less parallel to that of his own verse, verse which was already suggesting "elaborate form."

The mention above of "The Shadowy Waters" brings us to what is probably a more concrete and isolable influence of Mallarmé, Maeterlinck, and Villiers de l'Isle Adam on Yeats' poetry at the close of the nineteenth century—the return to myth-allegory in a more highly concentrated and densely symbolic form. In the decade intervening between the publication of "The Wanderings of Oisin" and the eventual appearance of "The Shadowy Waters," Yeats had published only one long work, his play "The Countless Kathleen"; instead his predilection had come to be more and more for the sort of short, neatly-rounded dramatic lyrics, varying between six and thirteen lines in length, which make up the majority of the poems in *The Wind Among the Reeds*. In 1894, however, Yeats had seen *Axël* in Paris, and had been inspired to renew efforts on his own long dramatic poem, the theme of which came to be remarkably similar to that of Villiers de l'Isle-Adam's play—in both cases great wordly wealth and consummate mortal love, symbolic of complete wordly contentment, are renounced in the search for a Platonically pure passion which represents the ultimate spiritual plateau.[17] The fact that these themes bear in turn a strong resemblance to that of Mallarmé's "Herodiade," in which the heroine deserts the world for a lonely tower where she can gradually evanesce into some mirrored essence, is evidence of the

---

[17] For a detailed discussion of the similarities between *Axël* and the second version of "The Shadowy Waters," see H. Goldgar, "*Axël* de Villiers de l'Isle Adam et The Shadowy Waters de W.B. Yeats," *Revue de Litt. Comparee*, XXIV, 563–574.

extent to which a strong community of interest bound Yeats to his French contemporaries.

The use of myth, as was pointed out above, was one final extension of symbolic technique of which the symbolists themselves greatly approved. A. G. Lehmann, however, is reluctant to give the status of "myth" to the works of Mallarmé and Maeterlinck, which he terms "pseudo-myths." He is particularly hard on the myths of the latter, which he feels lack the "allegorical" dimension—the capability of having "a general statement" extracted from "that formal element which we can pick out and isolate by calling it a 'plot'." [18] Such a view is puzzling in light of the ease with which a play like *Les Aveugles* lends itself to explication: the blind as sensorially-limited man, the dead priest as the church which has failed, the infant as the unspoiled primitive seer, and the last mysterious presence as the ultimate superhuman reckoning. This last element, of course, is difficult to bring out of ghostly vagueness, and it is this difficulty—so like that at the heart of Poe—which is a main point of weakness so far as Lehmann is concerned. Certainly Maeterlinck subdues his explicatory level far more than does Yeats, who not only had the advantage of an *established* mythology, but was perhaps more accustomed to the language of supernatural encounter. Forgael's speeches, for instance, perpetually point up the tension between human satisfaction and superhuman ambition which represents the allegorical element:

> I will have none of you.
> My love shakes out her hair upon the streams
> Where the world ends, or runs from wind to wind
> And eddy to eddy. Masters of our dreams,
> Why have you cloven me with a mortal love?

What really distinguishes "The Shadowy Waters" from most other symbolist dramas, however, is its correlation of a complex system of autonomous symbols with the basic myth-

---

[18] Lehmann, p. 297.

allegory. One might find some parallel in *Axël*, where Yeats had been impressed with Villiers de l'Isle-Adam's usage of the archetypal "lamp" and "tower," in addition to the thematic burden of the plot; [19] but the density, subtlety, and esotericism of Yeats' symbology render the play unique. What we really have here is a development and elaboration of that combination of myth and separate symbols which had appeared in "Oisin," where the allegory was studded with hornless deer, beech boughs, and other significant entities. The hornless deer and the hound appear again in the "The Shadowy Waters," but the latter is present in three different forms, all represented on Forgael's sail— red, dark, and white with red ears. Nor is this a nonce occurrence; each reappears as a motif in the play. Dectora, for instance, is said to have followed a red hound "for these nine years" (l. 268), and Mananan to have taken "a thousand women / When the dark hounds were loosed" (ll: 378–379). In a program note to the stage version written several years later, Yeats offers the unhelpful suggestion that the hounds may "correspond to the *Tamas*, *Rajas*, and *Sattva* qualities of the Vedanta philosophy." [20] Other symbols are multiplied accordingly; there are ubiquitous sea-birds, representing the souls of the dead in various stages, and a catalogue of ancient Irish animal symbols— including a flower, bird, fish, and morning star—which symbolize the hero Forgael (11. 424–428).

Ellmann is unquestionably correct in affirming that "The Shadowy Waters" represents "the farthest range of symbolism in dramatic poetry in English until the twentieth century," and as such it is a landmark.[21] The next century, however, as Ellmann's statement implies, would see a significant expansion of the symbol's possibilities in the work of Yeats and others. Yeats himself had realized, a few years earlier, that another and more

[19] See Yeats' introduction to H.P.R. Finberg's translation of *Axël* (London, 1925), pp. 7–11.
[20] Quoted by Ellmann in *Identity*, p. 81.
[21] *Identity*, p. 84.

absolute limit was being reached, and asked and answered in magnificent rhetoric:

> After Stéphane Mallarmé, after Paul Verlaine, after Gustave Moreau, after Puvis de Chavannes, after our own verse, after all our subtle colour and nervous rhythm, after the faint mixed tints of Condor, what more is possible? After us the Savage God. (A, p. 210)

Yeats' "Savage God" here is the ultimate extension of that "comic objectivity" so alien to tragedy, but it is amusing to think that it was a Savage God of another sort who made his appearance in Yeats' own poetry in the early decades of the next century, putting an end to Maeterlinckian anemia. His approach was first heralded in the colloquial overtones of *In the Seven Woods*, and by the time of the "Crazy Jane" poems, his reign was undisputed.

V

Epilogue

THIS IS NOT THE PLACE TO RE-WRITE THE STORY of Yeats' striking development into a "modern" poet during the early decades of the twentieth century, but a brief survey of the forms which the tendencies traced above eventually took may be helpful by way of epilogue. Certainly Yeats remained in some sense a "Romantic" through his entire career, a fact indicated by the quotation from "Coole Park and Ballylee" which opened the first chapter, and reinforced in his last volume of poetry by "High Talk," where he envisages himself alternately as "Malachi Stilt-Jack" and "A barnacle goose / Far up in the stretches of night." It is the elevation of his artistic focus and of his subject matter with which he is concerned here, and with his role as diminished but determined heir to the great tradition:

> What if my great-granddad had a pair that were twenty foot
> high,
> And mine were but fifteen foot, no modern stalks upon higher.

Actually, Yeats saw most fellow moderns stalking about with no stilts at all, losing elevation through their preoccupation with the prosaic and the accidental, and through their passive role as recorders; thus he writes in the introduction to the *Oxford Book of Modern Verse*:

> It has sometimes seemed of late years . . . as if the poet could at any moment write a poem by recording the fortuitous scene or thought, perhaps it might be enough to put into some fashionable rhythm—'I am sitting in a chair, there are three dead flies on a corner of the ceiling.' (p. xxviii)

Opposed to such poetry was that which dealt with the essential and permanent, and which represented the attempt of the poet to fashion an attitude of heroic control, or at least of heroic aspiration. The fact that Yeats' first presentations of this attitude occur in the daemonic encounters of such heroes as Oisin and the knight of "The Seeker" leads us to realize that the poet sensed a connection between his late, private usage of the term "Romantic" to mean something like "partaking of heroic grandeur" and the more conventional usage which emphasizes—among other things—the supernaturalism of Shelley, Keats, and Byron. It is not surprising that, for a poet of Yeats' peculiar bias and background, the most obvious arena of elevation would be found in the zone where man confronts the unknown forces of the cosmos; or that such a poet, in a period of his life when Romantic and Elizabethan influences were closely interwoven, should settle upon what might be called "daemonic tragedy" as the ultimate genre for the elevation which he desired.

This link between "Romanticism" and "tragedy" in Yeats' mind is important in a consideration of the continuity of his career. The distance from the inflated pathos of "Time and the Witch Vivien" to the Nietzschean tragic laughter of such late poems as "The Gyres" and "Lapis Lazuli" seems at first to make the connection of the two periods represented a tenuous thing; Vivien's fear of entering "the bloodless land / Among the whimpering ghosts" is hard to reconcile with Yeats' eventual realization that ". . . Hamlet and Lear are gay; / Gaiety transfiguring all that dread." Nonetheless, despite the increase in maturity and subtlety in Yeats' conception of tragedy, the impulse toward the high tragic plateau and the intuition of a remote and ultimate tragic attitude even beyond triumphant gaiety are remarkably constant throughout his career. As the counterpart of the shadowy giants and the statues of the Eighties, with their lack of delineated comic detail, we have the namesakes of "The Statues," written a year before Yeats' death:

> Pythagoras planned it. Why did the people stare?
> His numbers, though they moved or seemed to move
> In marble or in bronze, lacked character.
> But boys and girls, pale from the imagined love
> Of solitary beds, knew what they were,
> That passion could bring character enough,
> And pressed at midnight in some public place
> Live lips upon a plummet-measured face.

As in "The Wanderings of Oisin," written half a century earlier, Yeats is concerned with that altitudinous point at which character is transcended, and the dross of humanity is purified into the clean lineaments and essentials of a superhuman Platonic reality. The difference, of course, is that this conception, instead of being vitiated by "yellows and greens," is rendered more striking through the use of an unbridled vocabulary, and through occasional stark contrasts with the "foul rag-and-bone shop" at the other extreme of existence.

The tendency toward the dramatization of the lyric also continued in Yeats' work, as evidenced by the constant appearance of addresses, imperatives, and the framework of prayer; and even of extended dialogues such as "Shepherd and Goatherd," "Ego Dominus Tuus," and "The Hero, the Girl, and the Fool." Perhaps more significant, however, is the merger of this tendency with that toward the mode of the daemonic in what might be called the "internalizing" of the encounter between man and the supernatural. Witches and superhuman "Powers" were replaced to a great extent by "images," "thoughts," the "anti-self," and other mental phenomena which represented Yeats' attempt to make a drama out of his own life, as the admirable Villon had done; thus various images hover in conflict with thoughts and with each other, and life is seen at times as a tension between "self" and "anti-self," at others as a tension between "Self" and "Soul." Man is still located heroically upon the frontier of familiar experience, at the intersection of myterious forces, but the frontier and the forces are more credible because they are seen as possessing an inner psychological validity independent of any sort of external reality. Most lyric poems are, of course, "thoughts" in some sense, but Yeats places his mental phenomena in perspective as such, partly by labelling them and partly by establishing a strong sense of the poet-persona in the condition which he so felicitously called "excited reverie." This latter technique, also important in the general dramatizing of the lyric, is evident everywhere among the later poems: "I pace upon the battlements and stare. . . . "; "I climb to the towertop and lean. . . . "; "I meditate upon a swallow's flight"; "I turn away and shut the door and on the stair / Wonder. . . . "

The importance of this "reverie" as a dramatic process in Yeats' later verse is underscored by the fact that two of his finest poems, "Among School Children" and "Byzantium," are basically dramas of thought and image. In the former, the exterior scene of the schoolroom merely serves as a catalyst to thought, and the second stanza marks a switch to the mental arena: "I dream of a Ledaean body. . . . " Subsequently, the poet's mind is driven to such intense activity, particularly speculation, that the youthful image of a woman now withered with age seems to materialize with the vividness of physicality. Now begins a combat between this image and the present image—"Hollow of cheek as though it drank the wind"—which "floats into the mind," again emphasizing the mental orientation of the poem's basic conflict. Additional images are introduced *as images* in the "shape" which animates the mother's "reveries" with a picture of her youthful child, and in the icons worshipped by the nuns; and the power of these images is represented as something much more formidable than aesthetic effectiveness—they are able to "break hearts" and act as "mockers of man's enterprise" through floating into juxtaposition with the decrepitude of age. By calling the images "Presences" Yeats increases the sense of this ominous autonomy and gains a dramatic impact reminiscent of "the Rose," but without the incredibility of that earlier arcane symbol. Furthermore, the sense of autonomy is closely involved with the final movement of the poem toward the question of *which* image is that of ultimate reality, a question prepared for by the earlier reference to Plato's belief in nature as a mere "spume" and by the poignant incongruity of images of youth and age.

"Byzantium," concerned as it is with communicating the actual creative experience, is also involved in distinguishing between various phenomena of mental vision, and it opens with the recession of "the unpurged images of day"—the common prosaic images of everyday life. The presence of the poet-persona in a state of inspiration is then manifested in the second stanza: "Before me floats an image, man or shade." By ingenious gradations Yeats proceeds to the conclusion that the phenomenon is more spiritual than human, more mental than spiritual, yet partaking of all these in its complexity as an artistic image. The close relation between the thought-drama and the daemonic is evident in Yeats' salute to the "Breathless mouths" of the "superhuman," and one may suspect in this instance some lingering traces of the old belief that the symbol is the result of the "footsteps" of unseen "powers"; nonetheless, the "death-in-life and life-in-death" with which Yeats is dealing here is explicable in the cold but eternal qualities of "works of arts," in the sense of Keats' urn and Yeats' own golden singing bird. The poem ends with a picture of everyday concrete reality as a series of "images" which produces the "images" of art:

> Those images that yet
> Fresh images beget,
> That dolphin-torn, that gong-tormented sea.

The penultimate stanza of "Byzantium" is particularly interesting for its imagery, which represents the ultimate extension of the Shelleyan translucencies noted in Yeats' earliest verse and of the "pale" spiritistic conceptions of the Nineties. Here, however, far from suggesting the vitiation of *Weltschmerz*, the imagery bespeaks some seething Platonic energy which animates the mode of the daemonic and transcends the "mire" of physical detail for a direct approach to the *Anima Mundi*, the level of Yeatsian tragedy:

> Where blood-begotten spirits come
> And all complexities of fury leave,
> Dying into a dance,
> An agony of trance,
> An agony of flame that cannot singe a sleeve.

Similarly, in "Image from a Past Life," the annunciation of a daemonic image is prepared for by intricate patternings of light, which dissolve any sense of concrete normality:

> *He.* Never until this night have I been stirred.
> The elaborate starlight throws a reflection
> On the dark stream,
> Till all the eddies gleam. . . .

Obviously, the thought-drama has a close relation to the "vision" techniques which we have studied in relation to Yeatsian arcana of the Nineties, and it is not surprising to find that the technique is carried over into the later poetry without, of course, the esoteric apparatus which had accompanied it earlier. Highly reminiscent of "The Valley of the Black Pig" is "The Second Coming," which also deals with apocalypse. The opening "vision" of the later poem, however, is really more of an excited observation of the chaos which the poet actually sees about him. Access to supersensory sources occurs only when the excitement reaches a peak with the utterance of the archetypal phrase "The Second Coming," which unlocks the Platonic storehouse of the *Spiritus Mundi* to bring forth the terrifying sphinx image. Yeats handles the psychological machinery of vision here with an even surer hand than in "The Black Pig." The image emerges long enough for only a brief glance, and then "The darkness drops again." The aftermath is not an obscurantist turning to the "Master of the still stars," but a terrified mortal wondering about the vision's significance. Another striking use of vision occurs in lyric VIII of "A Woman Young and Old," where the visionary trance—itself archetypal in its derivation from the Adonis myth—is brought on by the heroine's staring at her bloodied fingernails while standing "At wine-dark midnight in the sacred wood."

As "The Second Coming" suggests, the Yeatsian symbol continued to retain some sort of relation to archetypal experience and the mode of the daemonic; the beast symbolic of an age lacking in mercy and pity is seen as an image from *Spiritus Mundi*. Symbols from traditional mythology appear with great frequency in Yeats' later poetry, often with suggestions of supernatural qualities. The tree of "Vacillation," for instance, "half all glittering flame and half all green," is modelled upon a tree from the medieval Welsh *Mabinogion*, and upon the Greek Attis festival. What is perhaps significant, however, is that the tree *symbolizes* a clearly defined metaphysical concept: the two halves of existence, spiritual and physical, which may be brought into reconciliation at some portentous half-way point. We see Yeats here coming around to a view of the symbol as a semantic vehicle while he retains the excitement and theatrical animation of daemonic suggestion, and the dramatic impact of particularity—this is, after all, "A" certain tree. The position may be regarded as one halfway between the French "figure of speech" view, with its representational component stressed at the expense of its aesthetic purport, and the Irish-arcane view, which reversed this emphasis. Mallarmé's "windows" are significant but dully general; Yeats' early "axle" and "Rose" vivid but obscure and non-representational. By the side of these, Yeats' later symbols seem to achieve some sort of desirable medium. "Byzantium" is easily generalized into "the process of artistic creation," even as the wealth of historical-legendary connotations of the city enhances the impact of the symbol itself, and as Yeats fills it with fiery translucent images of spiritual activity. Similarly, the tower at Gort, with its "winding stair," its stream full of moorhens outside, and its surrounding roads traversed by Irish irregulars usurps the eye of imagination entirely while retaining its basic symbolic suggestion of noble isolation, and awaking archetypal overtones reaching back through "Prince Athanase" to "Il Penseroso's Platonist."

The mention of "noble isolation" brings us to another aspect of Yeats' continued interest in the dramatization of the lyric—the persona modelled upon Elizabethan and Shelleyan examples. We have seen how the sorceresses and the haughty Coriolanean hero were merged into the arcane initiate of the Nineties; subsequently this figure is replaced in part by the figure of creativity, as examined in "Byzantium." The setting is often the symbolic tower, where the sense of isolation is dramatized through contrast with the active and dangerous life of passing soldiers or with the thought that the poet might have proved his worth "in something that all others understand or share." The conclusion, however, always justifies the solitary course with heroic certitude:

> The abstract joy,
> The half-read wisdom of daemonic images,
> Suffice the ageing man as once the growing boy.
> ("Meditations in Time of Civil War," VII)

The "tower-pose" is recognizable as a form of the "Ahasueruspose" which Yeats had singled out as an admirable example of Shelleyan "simplification through intensity." Now, without the complicating apparatus of the arcane or of purple island paradises, the "simplification" produced an effective impression of starkness more obviously related to intensity. We have not only the poet-persona as an example, but a succession of hermits and wanderers, including such figures as Ribh and Crazy Jane.

The contemplation of the former has brought him to an almost perpetual state of mystic vision, illuminated by the light of the Swedenborgian "intercourse of angels." [1] His dicta are couched not in the hazy terms of Rosicrucian and cabalistic doctrine, but in vigorous Blakean epithets "Godhead on Godhead in sexual spasm begot / Godhead"; "Hatred of God may bring the soul of God"; etc. [2] It is in the "Supernatural Songs" that the influence of Blake and his mystic predecessors becomes most vigorous, not during the earlier period when Yeats had edited Blake's poetry with Ellis.

One group of Yeatsian personae seem more exclusively descended from the Coriolanean hero. These are the contemporary Irish figures whose independence, aristocratic magnificence, and lofty spirits raise them above the common herd, which Yeats now brings in for effective contrast and in order to set up a basic tension of values in the poems. Thus Major Robert Gregory speaks first, in "An Irish Airman Foresees his Death," of what did *not* make him fight: "Nor law nor duty . . . Nor public men nor cheering crowds." This negative listing is extremely important in the animation of the Mask of cold simplicity, since it suggests the forcefulness and psychological energy necessary to suppress the myriad complexities which would make the pose's coherence and transcendence impossible. The "lonely impulse of delight," like the hedonistic simplification of Hemingway's heroes, must be seen to occur in a man who has rejected dull complication, not a man unaware of complication's existence. The actual achievement of the Airman's Mask —with its nonchalant sacrifice of life, its casual throwaway gesture—these represented for Yeats the final transcending of "character" necessary for translation to the level of tragic protagonist, and the poet even implies that these men are those at whom his verses are aimed:

[1] "Supernatural Songs," I.
[2] "Supernatural Songs," II and III, respectively.

> . . . call those works extravagance of breath
> That are not suited for such men as come
> Proud, open-eyed and laughing to the tomb.
> ("Vacillation," III)

These personae are not always the speakers, of course; frequently Yeats is describing them in "excited reverie." One such example, "Beautiful Lofty Things," is of particular interest not only because it alludes to Lady Gregory and Maud Gonne, two of the most frequent Coriolanean heroines, but because it shows Yeats' continued usage of the gesture and attitude which he had partly learned from the Pre-Raphaelites:

> Beautiful lofty things: O'Leary's noble head;
> My father upon the Abbey stage, before him a raging crowd:
> 'This Land of Saints,' and then as the applause died out,
> 'Of plaster Saints'; his beautiful mischievous head thrown back.
> Standish O'Grady supporting himself between the tables
> Speaking to a drunken audience high nonsensical words;
> Augusta Gregory seated at her great ormolu table,
> Her eightieth winter approaching: 'Yesterday he threatened
>   my life.
> I told him that nightly from six to seven I sat at this table,
> The blinds drawn up'; Maud Gonne at Howth station waiting a
>   train,
> Pallas Athene in that straight back and arrogant head:
> All the Olympians; a thing never known again.

Contrasted with the "raging" of the "crowd" is the defiant yet nonchalant pose of Yeats' father, who delivers an offhanded thrust in a manner strikingly similar to that of Coriolanus besieged by malicious servants in the house of Aufidius. Augusta Gregory sits in state at a table which itself suggests nobility, and exhibits the same contempt for worldly fears as had her son Robert; while Maud Gonne is defined here only by her pose—"straight back and arrogant head"—bespeaking a hawklike spirit unsullied by the plebeian surroundings of a railroad station.

Among these heroic personae Yeats places the great Irish

statesmen—in particular Parnell—and the martyred Irish rebels who "weighed so lightly what they gave." [3] That such a placement should be made is a clue to the sort of aesthetic machinery which Yeats sets up for political themes in his later career. Ireland is raised to the level of a tragic arena, and the Gaels are seen as the inheritors of a proud, passionate spirit which belongs to an earlier and more heroic time, despite its modern fall into abeyance:

> We Irish, born into that ancient sect
> But thrown upon this filthy modern tide
> And by its formless spawning fury wrecked,
> Climb to our proper dark, that we may trace
> The lineaments of a plummet-measured face.

It is perhaps significant that this passage occurs in "The Statues," for an interesting parallel emerges. Just as the great sculptured figures transcend "character" in suggesting the level of the *Anima Mundi*, so the aspect of Ireland which Yeats attempts to capture is some sort of spiritual essence beyond the brute realities of political squabbling, and beyond the raw, naive patriotic sentiments which had marred the Young Ireland volume of 1888. Yeats, who had earlier acknowledged Lionel Johnson's superiority in the verse of "political thought" and had guided his own nationalism in the artistically "safer" direction of mythology, now comes to feel confident to deal with political matter susceptible to sentimental and propagandistic pitfalls because he now feels capable of extracting and concentrating upon the cold aesthetic quintessence of the matter. This capability is verified by the magnificent "Easter 1916," where the leaders of the Easter Rising acquire tragic stature by resigning their role in "the casual comedy" in favor of the "terrible beauty" of an ultimate and unstinting personal sacrifice. (Note again the use of "comedy" to characterize the idiosyncratic, mundane level of existence opposed to the depersonalized tragic level.) Again,

[3] "September, 1913."

Parnell is contrasted with the "loose-lipped demagogues" who court hoi polloi, and is viewed instead as an Ahasuerus-like student of the *Anima Mundi*:

> Their school a crowd, his master solitude;
> Through Jonathan Swift's dark grove he passed, and there
> Plucked bitter wisdom that enriched his blood.

Even the deceptively simple political ballads of Yeats' last years depend upon this tragic sense; "Grandfather" sings a song of gay defiance while standing "under the gallows" in the first of "Three Songs to the Same Tune," and "Come Gather round me Parnellites" depends upon perception of a slightly ethnicized version of the man who passed through "Jonathan Swift's dark grove":

> Every man that sings a song
> Keeps Parnell in his mind.
> For Parnell was a proud man,
> No prouder trod the ground,
> And a proud man's a lovely man,
> So pass the bottle round.

If this is simplicity, it is not that of the Young Ireland ballads but the complex mask of "simplification through intensity" which is the result of long artistic labor rather than actual spontaneity, and which renders the "cold eye" of Yeats' epitaphic horseman something infinitely more active and complicated than mere indifference.

Select Bibliography

Allingham, William. *Irish Songs and Poems*. London, 1887.

Alspach, R.K. "Some Sources of Yeats's The Wanderings of Oisin," *PMLA*, LVIII (1943), 849–866.

Bjersby, Birgit. *The Interpretation of the Cuchulain Legend in the Works of W.B. Yeats*. Upsala, Sweden, 1950.

Bloom, Harold. *Yeats*. Oxford, 1970.

The Book of the Rhymers' Club. London, 1892.

The Book of the Rhymers' Club. London, 1894.

Bornstein, George. *Yeats and Shelley*. Chicago, 1970.

Curtis, Edmund. *A History of Ireland*, 6th ed. London, 1950.

Curtin, Jeremiah. *Myths and Folklore of Ireland*. London, 1890.

Ellmann, Richard. *The Identity of Yeats*. London, 1954.

_____. *The Man and the Masks*. New York, 1958.

Engelberg, Edward. *The Vast Design: Patterns in W.B. Yeats' Aesthetic*. Toronto, 1964.

Goldgar, J. "Axel de Villiers de l'Isle Adam et *The Shadowy Waters* de W.B. Yeats," *Revue de Litt. Comparee*, XIV (1950), 563–574.

Grierson, B.J.C. *Lyrical Poetry from Blake to Hardy*. London, 1928.

Grossman, Allen. *Poetic Knowledge in the Early Yeats*. Charlottesville, 1969.

Gurd, P. *The Early Poetry of W.B. Yeats*. Lancaster, Pa., 1916.

Hoare, Dorothy. *The Works of Morris and Yeats in Relation to Early Saga Literature*. Cambridge, 1937.

Hone, J.N. *W.B. Yeats, 1865–1939*. New York, 1943.

Hough, Graham. *The Last Romantics*. London, 1949.

Jackson, Kenneth. *Studies in Early Celtic Nature Poetry*. Cambridge, 1935.

Jeffares, A. Norman. *W.B. Yeats: Man and Poet*. London, 1949.

Johnson, Lionel. *Poetical Works*. New York, 1915.

Lehman, A.G. *The Symbolist Aesthetic in France, 1885–1895*. Oxford, 1950.

Mackail, J.W. *The Life of William Morris*. 2 vols. London, New York, and Bombay, 1899.

Meyer, Kuno, and Alfred Nutt. *The Voyage of Bran*. London, 1895–1897.

Moore, Virginia. *The Unicorn*. New York, 1954.

Orel, Harold. *The Development of William Butler Yeats*. Lawrence, Kansas, 1968.

Parkinson, T. *W.B. Yeats, Self Critic*. Berkeley, 1951.

Poems and Ballads of Young Ireland. Dublin, 1888.

Ransom, John Crowe. *The New Criticism*. Norfolk, Conn., 1941.

Stewart, J.I.M. *Eight Modern Writers*. Oxford, 1963.

Tindall, W.Y. "The Symbolism of W.B. Yeats," *Accent*, V (Summer, 1940), 203–211.

Transactions of the Ossianic Society, for the Year 1856, IV. Dublin, 1859.

"The Wanderings of Oisin and other Poems." Anon. rev., *Manchester Guardian*, Jan. 28, 1889.

Welby, T.E. *The Victorian Romantics*. London, 1929.

Wilson, Edmund. *Axel's Castle*. New York, 1931.

Yeats, W.B. *The Autobiographies*. New York, 1953.

_____. (ed.) *A Book of Irish Verse*. London, 1895.

_____. *Essays and Introductions*. London, 1961.

_____. *Fairy and Folk Tales of the Irish Peasantry*. London, 1888.

_____. *The Letters*, ed. Allan Wade. London, 1954.

_____. *Mythologies*. London, 1959.

_____. (ed.) *The Oxford Book of Modern Verse*. Oxford, 1936.

_____. *The Secret Rose*. London, 1897.

_____. *A Tribute to Thomas Davis*. Oxford, 1947.

_____. *The Variorum Edition of the Poems*, ed. Allt and Alspach. New York, 1957.

_____. *A Vision*. London, 1962.

Index